BY THE SAME AUTHOR

JIM CLARK
The Legend Lives On

WHY FINISH LAST?
The story behind the London–Sydney Marathon

ECURIE ECOSSE
A social history of motor racing from the 50's to the 90's

As part of our ongoing market research, we are always pleased to receive comments about our books, suggestions for new titles, or requests for catalogues. Please write to: The Editorial Director, Patrick Stephens Limited, Sparkford, Nr Yeovil, Somerset, BA22 7JJ.

Reg Parnell

The quiet man who helped to engineer
Britain's post-war motor racing revolution

GRAHAM GAULD

Patrick Stephens Limited

To Jane for perseverance

First published in November 1996

British Library Cataloguing in Publication Data:
A catalogue record for this book is available from the British Library

ISBN 1 85260 561 8

Library of Congress catalog card no. 96 75830

Patrick Stephens Limited is an imprint of Haynes Publishing, Sparkford, Nr Yeovil, Somerset, BA22 7JJ.

Typeset by J. H. Haynes & Co. Ltd
Printed and bound in Great Britain by
Biddles Ltd, Guildford and King's Lynn

Contents

Foreword

TO FOLLOW IN the footsteps of a famous father is never easy. I grew up knowing of my father's successes and failures and I ventured along a similar path which created problems in my own racing career. Expectations were high and criticism would be swift.

My father was a strong, tough character. With me he was always very demanding and he was always trying to teach me the value of money and insisting that civility cost nothing. I often used to smile when he was rollicking Roy Salvadori, because he thought a lot of Roy having been with him for many years in his racing life. Roy became like an older brother to me and like Roy I used to get a rollicking from my father every Sunday lunchtime when he was at the farm; but really it was only to make us better men.

He gave me a wonderful education at Oakham boarding school, mainly because he had not had such an opportunity himself.

What really came home to me after my father's untimely death, was the esteem in which he was held all over the World. People would go out of their way to talk to me about his achievements, his generosity and his friendliness. I began to think more deeply about his character, his successes and failures as well as about the challenges which he faced in his personal life and during that particular era in motor racing.

At an early stage in his life he recognised his talent for motor racing and with his very astute mind he seized the opportunity to acquire the cars which would give him a chance to compete in this fascinating sport.

This book will tell you the story of a determined, ambitious man who worked so very hard to establish a successful career, who made mistakes, who displayed great loyalty, who nurtured talent in others and who died far too soon leaving me a challenging example I still try to follow.

I remember my father once telling me of Raymond Mays' visit to Sir Stafford Cripps, the then Chancellor of the Exchequer in the immediate post-war Labour Government, at 11 Downing Street pleading for special steels for the BRM cars and this was duly given. In fact another great motor sporting figure of the time, Dennis Flather of Sheffield, was able to provide these under licence to the BRM project.

The result of this was the development of the kind of British engineering which has seen us dominate racing car design and development for the past thirty years. I often wonder what my father would have thought of it all today because the real revolution had not yet started when he died.

Times have changed and I am proud to know that my father played a part in that change.

R. H. H. (Tim) Parnell
Ashby de la Zouch.
April 1996.

Author's Introduction

TO RACING ENTHUSIASTS of the early post-war period the name of Reg Parnell needs no introduction, but how might he best be introduced to enthusiasts today? Well, one way would be to present the Parnell story with a modern slant, with greater news emphasis on the negative than the positive. Thus the fact that Reg Parnell was hauled up before the RAC and stripped of his racing licence *sine die* – which, on the face of it, meant that he could never race again – might appeal to their sense of the bizarre. Then again, the manner in which he hoarded racing cars throughout the Second World War as a speculative gesture might be seen as a brave modern entrepreneurial coup. That he was the only British driver ever to be selected to race with the all-conquering factory Alfa Romeo Grand Prix team might also be of interest. That he had a wry sense of humour and a devastating facility for fooling people might also be of interest.

But it is a tough job reaching out across the generations. The world has changed a lot, and although today grand prix racing and the World Championship has risen to become almost an obsession close to football, that doesn't change the fact that pioneers like Reg Parnell helped shape it in those early days after the war. If more of today's enthusiasts were to explore what happened in the past, they might not be too surprised at what happens today, for much of it is an extension of what Reg Parnell and others were doing 40 years ago.

Parnell was often accused of being a 'wheeler-dealer'; by today's standards and definition this could imply that he was a crook, but by the standards of the 1950s and '60s he was just 'sharp'. A fellow farmer/racing driver, Henry Taylor, adds weight to this definition: 'He was a farmer, and we all wheeled and dealed – we all walked about with cash in our back pockets because that's what farmers did. We didn't write cheques because farming life is a different world. Of course it is a bit different again now, but essentially a farmer is a wheeler-dealer whether he is buying pigs, cabbages or racing cars.'

This is one of the toughest books I have ever tackled because very few people knew much about Reg Parnell, and the journalists of the day seemed to have been put off by this gruff-voiced Derbyshire farmer who bucked the system in more ways than one. He was harshly penalised at Brooklands partly because he was 'from the other side of the tracks', yet he negotiated his way through the immediate post-war currency restrictions with remarkable facility.

He had a great eye for racing talent and had a particular interest in motor cycle racers. He certainly encouraged John Surtees, who eventually was to drive for him; likewise Mike Hailwood, who was to become a partner with Reg in his racing team. He was instrumental in bringing Chris Amon to Europe, and was the first person to sign Jim Clark to a grand prix contract – when he could not supply an Aston Martin for him in 1960, Reg was happy to let Clark sign for Colin Chapman and Lotus.

Thankfully Reg was survived by his only son, Tim, who is one of the great characters of motor racing and who rightly deserves a chapter to himself at the end of the book. Like his father, Tim is a farmer and also raced right up to Formula 1, but was not encouraged in his early days. Today he is on the Board of the British Racing Drivers' Club, and I am indebted to him for the time he has given to recall the Parnell story and for sorting out some of the different elements within Reg's life. I am also indebted to many other people, who are listed below, and apologise to those with whom I have had many conversations over the past year, but who may have been left out.

There was one hilarious evening in rural Leicestershire with Tim Parnell and Chris Ashmore as they talked about the wheeling and dealing done by their respective fathers. Joe Ashmore, father of Chris and Gerald, was a kenspeckle character who, with his brother Fred, was a business partner of Reg Parnell. With his normal dress of open-neck shirt and trousers held up by braces, Joe was hardly the kind of chap you would associate with the higher echelons of the sport, but after the war he set out for Switzerland with Reg and Rob Walker to try and buy one of the legendary 1939 1.5 litre supercharged Mercedes Benz racing cars from former driver Rudi Carraciola. Joe even had the cheque in his pocket, but the American authorities immediately after the war had something to say about this, and the dynamic trio came back empty-handed. Then there was the story about one of the two Maserati 4CLTs that Reg and Joe owned, which went back to Italy and mysteriously disappeared, never to be heard of again; but then things like that happened in those days.

Earlier I mentioned about Reg Parnell being banned from racing in 1938, and I am indebted to Neil Eason Gibson and the RAC Motorsport Division, first for looking out the specific minutes of the Competitions Committee when they ruled on Reg's ban, and then for giving me permission to publish the extracts verbatim; also to Diana Gaze, widow of the late Lex Davison, for copies of some of Lex's 'lively' correspondence with Reg; but most of all to Gillian Stillwell, who was Reg's long-time Secretary at Aston Martin and at Reg Parnell Racing, and who now lives in Australia with her husband, former racing driver Bib Stillwell. Gillian even sent me her meticulously hand-written test session notes, which revealed much interesting information about the original test drives given to both John Surtees and Jim Clark.

There are many more people who have helped to fill in the gaps and chasms that existed in Reg Parnell's life. One is Tony Gaze, the Australian driver who used to race in Britain with Alta, HWM and Maserati cars, and later had a Ferrari 500, and who travelled with Reg during his Tasman series with the original single-seater Aston Martin prototype. Another is the legendary photographer Louis Klementaski, who not only undertook two Mille Miglias sitting beside Reg in Aston Martins, but also competed in the Monte Carlo Rally as Reg's co-driver, also in an Aston Martin. This gentle and polite man, now living in retirement near Bath and writing his own memoirs, has a remarkable memory for detail, and I am grateful to him for his impressions of those races with Parnell.

This, then, has been something of an adventure, for although I watched Reg Parnell race from the early 1950s, I never actually met him. This was par for the course for most journalists of the time, or so it seems, for very little in the way of contemporary articles was written about him. Such reports as were published in books and magazines referring to races in which he competed at times conflict with each other, and I am conscious of the fact that there were occasions when I had to adopt the 'eeny meeny miney mo' principle of historic evaluation.

So in the end, what have we? In this introduction I have tried to give the reader some idea of what is to follow. It is a book about a driver who spanned two very different eras, the elegant, class-conscious period of Brooklands – and the less class-conscious pre-war Donington and Crystal Palace events – and the great leap forward for British motor racing after the war. While others forged ahead with the

500 cc movement, bringing inexpensive motor racing to the masses, Reg Parnell always sought to bring Britain more closely into the international racing system and find a British grand prix winner. He tried it himself with his Challenger, and later with the still-born Parnell, then hacked away at the original BRM and gave the ill-fated car its first ever race win. He even raced an early Connaught only to see Tony Brooks achieve its greatest success at Syracuse in 1955, which set the stage for the domination of motor racing by British teams that has been seen to this day.

Reg Parnell was no Jim Clark or Alain Prost; his driving style before the war verged on hooliganism, and he paid the penalty for it. He had none of the finesse and glamour surrounding Stirling Moss. He was a good journeyman racing driver who, when he was given the goods, always delivered. Indeed, when Alfa Romeo gave him a factory drive in a Type 158, they even de-tuned the car to make sure that he did not embarrass the regular team drivers – yet at the end of the race he was right behind them and ahead of everyone else.

I would like to acknowledge the help and support given by the following people, as well as the printed sources, without which this book would have remained unwritten:

Chris Ashmore, Gerald Ashmore, Hans Berends (Switzerland), Tony Brooks, Harry Calton and Roger Stowers (Aston Martin), John Coombs, Nick Cussins, Alan Dakers, Diana Gaze, Tony Gaze, Neil Eason Gibson, Ken Gregory, Louis Klementaski, Alain Mathat (France), Doug Nye, Tim Parnell, Tony Robinson, Roy Salvadori, John Surtees, Gillian Stillwell, Henry Taylor, Eric Thomson, Rob Walker, Ian Scott Watson, and Rob Young (South Africa).

Finally, in some places the starting money of the 1940s and '50s is shown with a second figure in brackets, being a rough indication of the value of the amount in today's terms.

Graham Gauld
St Paul en Foret
France
March 1996

Prologue

THE YEAR IS 1927 and somewhere in the town of Derby a private bus has been stopped by a policeman.

'How old are you?' he asks the driver.

'Just gone 21,' snaps the fair-haired youth behind the wheel.

'Now look, sonny,' replies the constable, 'We know all about you. 'You're fifteen and a half, and in case you want to know a Trent bus driver just reported you to us – but we're not going to do anything about it.'

The driver was Reginald Parnell, but what the policeman didn't know was that a year or so earlier, when Reg's brother Bill had been stuck for a lorry driver, he had told Reg that he had to drive. Reg had protested, saying that he was only just 14 and couldn't drive! So his brother had told him to get into the cab and drive the lorry round the main square in Derby. When Reg managed to complete this task without hitting anything, his brother said, 'That was good driving – now you know how to drive, take this lorry to Grantham!'

Those were the 1920s, and motor racing in England was concentrated on the Brooklands Circuit near Weybridge, Surrey, where the right crowd met and there was certainly no crowding. Motor racing was for the elite or the gifted, and was not yet ready to welcome a lorry driver from Derby. Not that the idea had entered Reg Parnell's head back in those days – he had other things to think about.

From lorries Reg moved on to buses as a driver in the family transport business, which led to the incident described above. It gives a quaint picture of the tranquillity of life in those days, and the tolerance of the police, for Parnell continued to drive lorries and buses until he was old enough to get a legal licence!

Working in the family business meant that his education suffered, but although he never really went to school in his late teens, he was fascinated by engineering.

His parents were tenants of a pub in Derby, the Royal Standard, which had stables at the back. When the local drovers arrived in town for the Derby cattle market, they used to sleep in the stables the night before. Reg's sister Alice recalled leaving school at about 13, and her first job at the pub was cleaning out the stables – not because the cattle were kept there, but because it was where the drovers slept.

The Parnell family was quite large. Alice was the oldest, then Bill – father of Roy Parnell who was later to become test driver with Aston Martin – Gladys, and finally the baby of the family, Reg. He left Gerrard Street School in Derby at the age of 12, and before long was roped into the haulage business, the Standard Transport Company, which his older brother Bill had started with a lorry, a bus and a charabanc.

The bus was bought because Bill had acquired a contract to drive the workmen for the British Celanese Company to and from work in Derby, while the charabanc was used to take people round the Peak District. Thankfully Reg, even at that age, was mechanically minded, and had plenty of work to do as breakdowns were frequent. On one occasion a lorry broke down on Shap Fell in Cumberland and Reg was stuck in the snow for four or five days before he could get the gearbox out, repair it and get the lorry back to Derby. Although Bill was the senior partner in the business, it was young Reg that worked hard on the mechanical side of the lorries to keep the business going.

Later Standard Transport Limited and the garage business, Standard Garage Company, were re-registered as the Standard Haulage Company, with a nominal capital of £6,000 and directors Bill, Reg and Alice Parnell, and George Baker, Reg's brother-in-law. (Baker's son Harold was killed as a little boy in a cycling accident, and when Reg's son Tim was born one week later he was given the name Harold as one of his middle names.)

Reg's father, Robert William Parnell, was a great football fan and became a shareholder in Derby County Football Club. Today his grandson Tim is a Vice-President of the club; indeed, he once made a bid to buy the ground, but was thwarted by Robert Maxwell. Tim remembers being taken by his father to the famous Cup Final at Wembley when Derby County won the cup. They went to the match with the then Chairman of the Club, Ben Robshaw, who was later to become a partner in Standard Haulage.

Now that he has retired from motor racing, does Tim Parnell want to move into the football limelight? 'I think the financing of football clubs is horrific – no, I just like to go to the Vice-Presidents' room and see my friends and don't want any drama. I used to go to the matches during my motor racing days just to sit and enjoy the games with my friends. I had enough drama with BRM to have to go through all that again with a football club . . .'

Chapter 1

1934-1937: The Motor Racing Bug Bites

WE ALL OF us tend to remember the first time that we saw racing cars in action. It is usually thrilling, not just because of the racing itself, but because of the atmosphere, the sounds, the smells and the people. For Reg Parnell that awakening took place in 1934 when the Donington Park racing circuit opened to the public. Donington was not far from Derby, so it was easy for Reg to visit.

In those days motor racing in Britain was very different from today. There was really only one major circuit in the country, Brooklands, and it was organised by people who had a more relaxed and private view of motor racing. It had been established in 1906 by a group of well-connected people, some of whom were members of the horse racing fraternity; even today the place in which the cars are stored is referred to as the 'Paddock'. Not only that, but a bell was rung before each race and some of the early drivers wore silks in the colours of the car's owner if he was involved in horse racing too.

By 1934 Brooklands was therefore well established as a traditional place for gentlemen's racing, and, as Reg Parnell was to find out a few years later, they played to the rules of gentlemen and amateurs. It could be said that the influence of Brooklands, and this emphasis on a variety of types of racing and handicapping, kept Britain out of the development of the international system of classes and divisions that was prevalent in European international motor racing at that time. This, however, was to change dramatically after the Second World War, and Reg Parnell was in the vanguard of that change – but we run ahead of ourselves.

Donington Park had arrived on the scene thanks to the Derbyshire Motor Cycle & Sports Car Club, led by Gillie Shields, who was the bailiff at Donington. Eventually he bought Donington Park from the family who owned it, and he and the legendary Fred Craner went on to develop racing there. When the first race took place in 1934 it created a whole new interest in motor racing in the Midlands and attracted huge crowds. Eventually it was to host the grand prix events at which Mercedes-Benz and Auto Union raced.

Picture that day at Donington Park in 1934, a circuit very different from the one we know today, with many more trees and a straight that ran past the site of the present Donington Collection. There was also a loop to the north of the existing paddock, which dropped down to a hairpin, then back uphill to the brow where the Mercedes-Benz and Auto Union racers of the late 1930s would buck and leap off the ground.

Parnell was fascinated, not only by the lure of speeding cars but by the fact that there was prize money to be won. This started him thinking about taking up motor racing, and he received some support from his brother Bill, who even went as far as to ask if he could drive a car on several occasions. Tim Parnell remembers: 'Bill wasn't much of a driver and in fact I think it made him quite ill at times, such as on the banking at Brooklands, which was terribly bumpy. The ride in those cars was very bad and some of the drivers had to wear a corset to hold themselves together. My Uncle Bill was not physically strong and was not as determined as Dad.'

Throughout his life Reg Parnell raced not only for fun but also for reward. This sport seemed like an easy and pleasant way to pick up some money, so he drew on his savings and invested £25 in an old 2 litre unsupercharged Grand Prix Bugatti. This he bought from Sam Hill, who had a scrapyard in Derby and was a distant relation whom Reg used to call Uncle Sam. Sam's salesman, Frank Radford, actually made the sale, and in the time-honoured tradition of racing car salesmanship he gave no sucker an even break! He recognised a novice when he saw one, and the car he sold Reg was a wreck.

Reg had a trailer and towed the Bugatti to its first and only outing at Donington behind an old Talbot. Before practice he sheared the diff just running round the paddock. He then learned his next lesson: if you drove a strange continental car back in those days, getting spare parts was a major problem, and when you eventually found them they cost a lot of money. He therefore quickly decided that the Bugatti had to go, and in its place he bought the car that was to bring him to the notice of everyone.

That car was an MG K3 Magnette. During the 1934 season many well-known drivers owned and raced these cars, some of them having special bodies fitted. The car that Reg Parnell bought was very special indeed, in today's terms the equivalent of buying one of last year's McLarens for GT racing.

The car had originally been bought by Hugh C. Hamilton, one of the best racing drivers of the day, and Hamilton had a very special off-set single-seater body fitted, with a cowl over the radiator, a head fairing and a long tapered tail. The engine was a supercharged 1,086 cc, and the car had a pre-selector gearbox as standard equipment. The basic K3 Magnette cost around £650, and it was a quick and very competitive car. Driving it in 1934 Hamilton won the small car race, run alongside the Coppa Acerbo in Pescara, Italy, and it was actually timed at over 122 mph over a kilometre, a remarkable performance for an 1,100 cc car back in those days.

Meanwhile Hamilton had been engaged by Whitney Straight, the American millionaire enthusiast (who was to become Chairman of BOAC after the war), to drive one of three Maseratis that Straight had bought for the 1934 season. The car was kept and maintained in Italy, while the other two came to Britain, had 'snowplough' noses added to them and raced successfully here. (One was subsequently sold to Prince Bira and today, more than 60 years later, it is still running well and appearing around the world raced by expatriate Briton Peter Giddings.)

In 1934 Hugh Hamilton was entered for the Swiss Grand Prix at Berne in the Straight Maserati, one of the mechanics for which was F. W. 'Lofty' England, later of Jaguar fame. Sadly Hamilton was killed in the race, and at the end of the season Bob Horton, a regular K3 Magnette racer, bought Hamilton's car from his family. It appears, however, that Horton never actually drove the car, but Reg Parnell got to hear of it and bought it for the 1935 season.

The presence of Rolls-Royce in Derby at that time meant the availability some of the finest engineers of the day, including Frank McEvoy, who was a genius when it came to supercharging and had helped to pioneer the Zoller supercharger. It was important to a young local racing driver to get the help of these people, and some of the Rolls-Royce engineers assisted Reg; indeed, they were known to make a few parts for Reg when he started racing seriously. It also helped that Melbourne Engineering was based beside Donington Park, and run by a Mr Allan who developed a twin-cam head for the MG Magnette. He was also to help Reg Parnell when he decided to build his own grand prix car, the Challenger, many years later.

The first record of Reg racing the car was in the second race meeting of the season at Donington on 11 May 1935. Fifty-one cars were entered for the meeting, and Reg ran in the five-lap event for cars up to 1,500 cc. The man to beat in his race was H. G. Dobbs in a Riley Special, but there were also other interesting names present. One was 'A. Bira', who was later to enter himself as 'B. Bira' and was later to be better known as Prince Bira of Siam. Bira's car was a Riley. Two other newcomers in the race were later to race in major events against Reg Parnell in the 1950s: Peter Walker, with a supercharged 1,100 cc Alta, and Horace Richards, driving another Riley.

For Reg it was very much the start of a long learning curve, and in its report of the race *Motor Sport* was obliged to mention that '. . . R. Parnell was not making an auspicious debut with the single-seater Magnette raced last season by the late H. C. Hamilton, which was running very slowly.' The magazine went on to report that '. . . One of the brightest spots in the race was the dashing driving of the Prince incognito "A. Bira" with his Riley Imp; he made up on the corners what he lacked in speed on the straight.'

Later in the season, and again at Donington, Reg entered for the Nuffield Trophy race over 60 laps and 150 miles. This was a handicap event and the entry also included Dick Seaman and Pat Fairfield in ERAs, but Seaman had to withdraw when the car ran a big-end in practice. H. C. Dobbs had a good start in the White Riley, but was followed off by Reg and Ashton Rigby in their Magnettes. Rigby got past Parnell, but right on his tail was Pat Fairfield in his ERA (remember that the little cars, of which Reg's was one, had a two-lap start). For Reg, however, there was no success, the Magnette retiring long before the end of the event.

Reg was, however, beginning to get to grips with the handling of the car, although its reliability was a different matter. At a later race meeting at Donington, Reg was having a tremendous battle with the similar Magnette of J. H. Smith and Peter Whitehead's Alta when Richard Bolster – brother of commentator and racing driver John Bolster – spun at Red Gate. Smith, Whitehead and Parnell swerved to avoid Bolster, all three of them going on to the grass but managing to avoid a photographer who was standing at the edge of the track terrified as racing cars passed him on either side.

(*I know how terrifying this can be – I was standing on a straw bale on the outside of the hairpin at the Kirkistown circuit in Ireland at the 1953 500 cc Championship of Ireland when Ken Tyrrell, driving a Cooper 500, braked too late and shot out of control straight towards my straw bale, just managing to avoid me. Some 20 years later at a social gathering I admitted this to Ken, and his reply was '. . . so you were the stupid bastard on that straw bale!'*)

At this same Donington Race meeting Reg loaned his car to his brother Bill who was entered as 'J.' Parnell and was the scratch man for the race. Later in the afternoon, to complete a successful day, Reg came out in the ten-lap handicap event for cars up to 3.5 litres and scored his first ever motor racing victory.

Up to that time, and in his later races, Reg was not exactly the tidiest driver; he was always quoted as being wild, but one contemporary report recorded that '. . . Parnell was fairly streaking through the field. This time no one could possibly find fault with his driving, which was really quick and at the same time controlled. We shall hear a lot more of Parnell in the future for he obviously has a flair for the game. On the seventh lap he took the lead and was not headed for the rest of the race.' Sadly, Reg's reputation for wild driving was to catch up with him two years later, as we shall see.

The first big race over a real road circuit in Britain organised by an independent club, the British Racing Drivers' Club's British Empire Trophy at Donington, took place on Saturday 4 April 1936. It was won by Dick Seaman driving a 2.6 litre supercharged Maserati from Pat Fairfield's ERA and W. G. Everitt's Alfa Romeo. There was a tremendous entry for the event, including one 'W. Parnell' (sic) driving a 1,400 cc supercharged MG. He was not to finish, but he completed 60 laps before the car expired.

Later in the year Reg returned to Donington for the Nuffield Trophy, with the main race covering 60 laps on handicap for cars up to 1,500 cc. It gave him another chance to show his skill, but part way through the race, as he rushed down to Starkey's Corner, his nearside front wheel sheared off, and although he took to the grass he was able to bring the car to a stop without much damage. Unfortunately he could not continue as the wheel had taken the brake drum with it.

In the Junior Car Club Donington '200' he managed to finish 8th, but was five laps behind the winner. However, as Raymond Mays with his ERA was seventh, people were beginning to notice the flamboyant and sometimes wild local driver from up the road in Derby.

While wandering through the paddock at this meeting he found one of the local competitors in trouble with his car. His name was Joe Ashmore, a local motor dealer; Reg helped him out with his magneto and they became firm friends. Later Joe and his brother Fred would join forces with Reg to found Highfield Garages, which was the repository for all the racing cars that had been sold off during the war.

The Ashmores were a wild bunch, as Chris Ashmore, one of Joe's sons, recalls: 'My Uncle Fred ran off when he was a young lad and got involved with the travelling show people. He was a great man for fights and could pick a fight with anyone. In those days they used those big steam traction engines with an outside flywheel and belt to drive all the roundabouts at the showground and Uncle Fred had the job of running one of these. One night he felt like having a drink, so guessing that there was enough water in the boiler to last an hour or so, he nipped off. Unfortunately he had miscalculated and the engine and all the fairground rides stopped, so he was kicked out.'

Chris Ashmore and his older brother Gerald (Gerry) were regular competitors in the 1960s, Chris first with an Austin Healey 100S, a Formula Junior Lotus 20 and an aged Cooper Formula 1 car, while Gerry was best known for racing a D-type Jaguar. His car was XKD 510, which Duncan Hamilton had raced in the Dakar Grand Prix in 1956 and which he loaned to a young protégé of his, Tony Dennis. Dennis was tragically killed at Goodwood a month later, and the wrecked car was bought by Gerry. He then traded it with Neville Taylor in Barnsley for an Aston Martin DB3S, which led to an amusing incident. 'I drove the car back up the A38, and there were no speed limits in those days, and at about 90 mph I passed this Standard Vanguard estate car. When I got back home I wasn't happy with a noise in the engine, but then the phone rang and it was Ken Yates, a member of the BARC (British Automobile Racing Club) – he had been the man in the Vanguard.

'He immediately offered to buy the Aston, and as I wasn't sure about it I agreed to sell it to him and he went out to test it. At that time they had just opened the section of the M1 from the A45 to Hemel Hempstead, so I followed Ken and when he reached the M1 he shot off down the road in the Aston. He eventually got back at a crawl, and when we took the engine apart the crank was broken in three places. What had happened was that the former owner had packed the main bearings with silver paper, and of course I had no guarantee. My father Joe insisted that we put a new engine in for Ken, and he got in touch with Reg Parnell who was at Aston Martin at the time, and we got a reconditioned engine for £400 cash.

'The trouble was this happened the week before Ken was due to race, and I worked through Saturday night getting the car put together again. I remember Ken arriving about midnight with a packet of fish and chips, 50 fags and a bottle of cider just as I was attaching the flywheel. So I stopped, had the fish and chips then carried on. However, when Ken went out on the Sunday morning to try the car he came back with sparks from underneath, and I realised I hadn't tightened up the bolts on the flywheel! Eventually we managed to get the car to Goodwood for Ken to race on the Monday.'

The friendship between the Parnells and Ashmores has so far embraced two generations.

Another well-known motor racing character entered Reg Parnell's life around the mid-1930s, the small, affable, almost cocky Wilkie Wilkinson. Wilkie was to gain a huge reputation as a racing mechanic before the war, when he worked at Bellevue Garages preparing racing cars for the Evans brothers and their sister Doreen. This also gave Wilkie the opportunity to race cars, and he was a pretty capable driver if only because of his bravery. His meeting with Reg Parnell came about when the Evans family came to race at Donington and used Reg's garage to prepare their cars. The Evans' Bellevue Garage had assembled all the parts developed by Laurence Pomeroy and Frank McEvoy for the R-type MG; indeed, it was the Evans' MG R-type that was bought by Joe Ashmore to start his racing career, and Reg Parnell allegedly bought the twin-cam head design and the jigs. Many years later, after the war, the paths of Reg Parnell and Wilkie Wilkinson would again cross.

Finally at the end of that 1936 season there was the Donington Grand Prix, which brought a large entry that included the German driver Hans Ruesch, who shared his Alfa-Romeo with Dick Seaman. They were to win the event ahead of Charles Martin's Alfa Romeo. The winning Alfa was also to be a part of Reg Parnell's future, but that would not be until three years later. Reg ran well up the field, jousting with Peter Walker's ERA, but his exuberance overcame him again and at Starkey's Corner – which appeared to be his nemesis – he lost everything, shot across the grass at high speed and was lucky to catch the car and get back on to the track – but not for long, as the axle broke and he had to retire.

Perhaps as a result of this success Reg put in an entry for the Brooklands 500 Mile race at the end of the season, where he was up against all the big guns and multi-litre specials. It was a handicap event, as was the norm, but on this occasion the big cars were not handicapped out of it and John Cobb and Tim Rose Richards driving the Napier Railton were the winners. Reg, however, was towards the back of the pack fighting with a car that was not running well, and he eventually pulled in and retired with timing failure. He was to return to Brooklands a few weeks later and finish second in a Mountain race. By now the motor racing bug had well and truly bitten him, and he came to the conclusion to which most racing drivers come – he needed more power.

Over the winter of 1936 Reg got down to completely rebuilding the MG; he moved the steering to the centre to make it more of a single-seater, and new bodywork was designed to take advantage of this. He then approached the team of McEvoy and Pomeroy, who had designed a twin-overhead-camshaft head for MG Midgets, and asked them to design one for his Magnette. At the same time he enlarged the engine to 1,400 cc, and with the new twin-cam head the car became much more competitive.

During the 1937 season he ran at all the main events, including the new circuit at Crystal Palace, where ironically his racing career was virtually to come to an end in the 1950s.

There is no doubt that in those early days Reg Parnell was a pretty wild driver, and during a meeting on the Campbell Circuit at Brooklands in early July 1937 he was involved in another incident. Having passed Tuson's Ballila Fiat (it was a handicap event) into the lead, and with W. M. (Mike) Couper's Talbot right on his tail, Reg misjudged the corner at Vickers Bridge and went off the road. He swerved back on, forcing Couper's big Talbot into the bridge parapet, which broke its back axle. Reg won the race, but clearly his action had been noted.

On 17 July he ran J. H. T. Smith's Magnette at that year's second race meeting held at Crystal Palace. During practice the remains of the old Crystal Palace ruins – destroyed by fire the previous year – were blown up. Nobody had been told about this, so it must have come as a great surprise to the competitors when the explosion took place!

A young Bill Boddy, reporting the race in *Motor Sport*, painted a vivid picture of John Bolster's arrival with the rather hairy Bolster Special, which reflects some of the flavour and atmosphere of English racing at that time: 'John Bolster was another centre of attraction with the Bolster-Special "Mary" [*Motor Sport* was rather coy about publishing the car's real name, which was "Bloody Mary"]. We have the greatest respect for Bolster, who is proving that his quite unadorned, truly stark home-built cycle-car is as suited to road racing as to straight sprints. John's tennis shoes were even dirtier than those effected by the writer, while his flannels – well, they would never be tolerated at Weybridge [Brooklands]. But then we doubt whether "Mary" would be tolerated, either, though we should dearly love to see her in a Mountain race. Incidentally, how did Bolster get on over Supplementary Regulation 7c, calling for "an effective bulkhead between the driver's seat and the engine"? "Mary" has nothing like that; indeed, John still bandages his left elbow as protection from pipes and chains!'

Reg qualified on the front row of the grid, but as it was a handicap event this did not mean that he was one of the quickest. However, he took advantage of his position and led at the end of the first lap from Prince Bira's ERA. Bira quickly got past on the second lap, but Reg was driving as hard as he could, and in his usual rumbustious style. Arthur Dobson then got by with another ERA, but Parnell held on to finish 3rd. This meant that he was further handicapped for the final of what was called the London Grand Prix.

Thirteen drivers actually qualified for the final, but the organisers thought that as it was an unlucky number they should invite John Bolster – who had retired in the first heat – to run and make up the number. Once again Reg took the lead, but the heavily favoured drivers were catching up fast; Bira and Ian Connell in their ERAs finished first and second. Parnell meanwhile had his own battle with third-man Percy MacLure's Riley, and came in fourth. An interesting sidelight to this race is that Reg and Arthur Dobson both raced with crash helmets and visors, a relatively rare thing in those days.

A few weeks later Reg took part in one of his first major international races, the 200 Mile event of the Junior Car Club, which was a scratch event and run at Donington rather than at Brooklands. Again Parnell entered the MG, and the modifications he had made over the winter elevated him to being a true contender. He shared the fourth row of the grid with Charles Brackenbury in Austin Dobson's ERA, Hanson's Maserati and Tony Rolt in the 2.4 litre Triumph Dolomite.

On the opening lap Parnell was ninth ahead of Reggie Tongue's ERA and right behind Earl Howe (also ERA) and Brackenbury. He dropped back and was passed by Rolt, so with retirements he finished ninth, and last of the finishers. On this occasion the MG, trailing smoke from the cockpit, had clearly suffered problems, and Reg had a long pit-stop for fuel, water and plugs, during which he had time to get out and have a short stroll!

Chapter 2

1937-1939: Banned From Driving

THE 1937 RACING season ended badly for Reg Parnell, while he was practising for the BRDC '500' meeting at Brooklands on the fast Outer Circuit where average speeds were high. This was one of the major events of the year and Reg had entered his MG. On the Friday the weather was miserable, but he went out on the track to get as much practice as possible.

The brilliant woman driver Kay Petre had been offered a factory Austin Seven single-seater to race at the same meeting. She and Reg had enjoyed a great duel at Crystal Palace only a few weeks before, so both were aware of the other's ability. On this occasion, however, Kay Petre was still feeling her way in the Austin when she was overtaken by Reg high on the banking. The MG started to slide and Reg held it, but the loss of momentum caused the car to swerve down the banking and straight into Kay's car at right angles. The little Austin Seven rolled over and over, throwing Kay out on to the track. Perhaps it was fortunate that she was thrown clear, as the Seven was badly damaged and ended up in a ditch. Meanwhile Reg's MG careered off the track and into the railings, where he also sustained injuries, albeit minor compared to the petite and pretty Petre, who was rushed to the Weybridge Cottage Hospital with serious injuries.

Born Kay Defries, she was a Canadian and always something of a tomboy, despite being a small, very attractive and always well dressed woman with dark hair and a bubbly personality. She came to England and met her husband Henry Petre, one of the many pioneer pilots who flew out of Brooklands with his Deperdussin monoplane. He took part in air displays and was nicknamed Peter the Monk. Something of a character, and a noted male chauvinist, Henry had vowed never to have anything to do with women, and would even leave the local haunt, the Blue Bird cafe at Brooklands, if a girl appeared. Then one day he arrived with a young wife called Kay, who was quite happy to chatter away with the boys and become one of the gang.

She was determined to make a name for herself as a racing driver and started racing with an Invicta owned by her husband. However, Henry didn't like this idea and bought her a Wolseley Hornet in which she won her first Ladies Race at Brooklands. Not content with this, she persuaded one of Brooklands' legendary racing drivers, L. G. Hornstead – who had originally raced a Benz in 1911 – to teach her the rudiments of race driving, and in 1933 she bought a 2 litre supercharged Bugatti. Although she was very much 'one of the boys', she was also very feminine and used to choose her racing overalls to match the colour of the car. It is said that on one occasion, when her car was being overhauled, the seat was removed only to reveal a lipstick in a case, a stopwatch, seven cigarettes and various other things a woman might keep in a handbag – but these were lying in the undertray of a racing car!

In the impact of the Brooklands accident Kay Petre was knocked unconscious, but when they got her to hospital it was realised that she had very serious head injuries and her life was in the balance. However, she was a determined lady and not only survived the accident and some plastic surgery but even overcame partial paralysis. Needless to say it was one of her last races, but she had had a spectacular career.

Retiring from racing, she became motoring correspondent of the *Daily Sketch,* a post she held until after the war, when she was given a role within the Austin Motor Company as, amongst other things, their colour consultant. She was one of seven members of the motoring press who were present at an informal meeting at the Press Club in London on 9 October 1944, when plans were laid for a Motoring Correspondents' Circle – the forerunner of today's Guild of Motoring Writers.

The incident had repercussions for Reg Parnell, too, as a report had been prepared by the Stewards and sent to the RAC for consideration. More than two months went by before a brief announcement came from Pall Mall to say that the competition licence of Reginald Parnell had been permanently suspended from racing due to the accident involving Kay Petre. By that time she had completely recovered, and when asked about the penalty, journalists of the day were informed by the RAC that the press would not be given any information about the findings. There is one story that the Stewards at the meeting had detected alcohol on Reg's breath, but it should be pointed out that it was not uncommon in the sport to find people enjoying a drink. Indeed, in his biography Duncan Hamilton attributed part of his 1951 Le Mans win for Jaguar to Bols gin, while Ivor Bueb similarly kept a hip flask of brandy for Le Mans and one year Ken Wharton was seen to have a quick whisky before he stepped into the BRM at Silverstone. Bearing in mind the car, this latter may come as no surprise to anyone!

Tim Parnell totally refutes the drinking story: 'My father never started drinking until after the war, and was completely teetotal even though he was brought up in a pub. His father drank quite heavily, and I think that put him off.

'I was told that when he came back from the RAC hearing, his brother Bill told him he had better pack it up because "the Establishment will never accept you for what you are".'

I am indebted to Neil Eason Gibson of the RAC Motorsport Division – whose father, John Eason Gibson, was formerly Secretary of the British Racing Drivers' Club – who looked out and forwarded to me the relevant passages from the RAC Competitions Committee reports surrounding the incident; they read as follows:

Competitions Committee meeting Wednesday October 6 1937

Chairman: Colonel F. Lindsay Lloyd CMG CBE

Conduct of a Competitor
Arising out of an accident which occurred at Brooklands during the practising for the BRDC 500 Race, the Committee decided to hold an enquiry as to whether Mr R. Parnell is a fit person to hold an International Competition Licence. The enquiry to be held on Wednesday 27th October unless circumstances render it desirable to postpone it to a later date, and Mr Parnell to be given an opportunity to be present and to call witnesses.

Competitions Committee meeting Wednesday October 27 1937

Conduct of a Competitor
Preliminary discussion took place regarding the conduct of a certain competitor, and the question as to the responsibility for control of practising for the 500 kilometres race was raised. It was agreed that this point should be considered at a later meeting.

At 3.5 pm Mr R. Parnell was admitted with Mr Oliver Bertram, Counsel, instructed by Mr Lamborn of Crossman, Block & Co,

Solicitors. The Club Solicitor, and Mr D. J. Scannell, representing the British Racing Drivers' Club, were also present.

Evidence regarding Mr Parnell's driving record was submitted and Mr Parnell offered explanations of his various incidents referred to. He, with his Counsel, retired at 3.40 pm.

After considerable discussion it was agreed that the case should be adjourned to a later date for hearing further evidence.

Competitions Committee meeting Thursday November 11 1937

Conduct of a Competitor
A letter relating to the case of Mr R. Parnell from Lord Howe, together with the Secretary's reply thereto, was read and noted.

Mr Lionel Martin stated that as he desired to give evidence in this case he proposed to take no part in any deliberations or decisions that the Committee might come to.

At 2.45pm Mr R. Parnell was admitted with Mr Oliver Bertram, Counsel . . . The following witnesses were also present: Messrs Hugh P. McConnell, H. A. Hodge, J. R. Whittingham, R. R. Tanner and P. Maclure.

Evidence regarding Mr Parnell's driving record was continued from the previous hearing . . . Mr Parnell also made a statement on his own behalf and was examined thereon.

At 4.15 pm Mr Parnell with his Counsel and all the above witnesses, including Messrs L. Martin and L. Wilson, retired. After deliberation the committee decided that Mr Parnell should be suspended *sine die*, his suspension to date from November 11 1937.

At 4.55 pm Mr Parnell was re-admitted and informed of the Committee's decision. He thereupon gave notice of his intention to appeal against this decision to the Stewards of the Club, and then left the Committee. After consulting the terms of reference to the Competitions Committee, the Chairman ruled that Mr Parnell had the right to appeal to the Stewards, and it was agreed that Mr Parnell should be so advised forthwith.

Reg duly appealed and the hearing was held during the RAC Competitions Committee meeting of Wednesday 19 January 1938. The short note in the RAC records states: 'Conduct of a Competitor: It was reported that the appeal of Mr R. Parnell to the Stewards of the RAC against the decision of the Committee to suspend him *sine die* had now been heard and had been dismissed. A letter from Mr Parnell was read asking if he would be permitted to apply for a

Competition licence during 1938. The Committee declined to consider the matter.'

Even Kay Petre herself was quoted as saying that it was simply a racing accident, and she later made a personal appeal to the RAC for Reg's licence to be returned to him.

The RAC Competitions Committee meeting on 2 March 1938 reported: 'Matters arising: An application from Mr R. Parnell to hold a Competitor's licence was considered and refused.'

It was said at the time that the RAC had based their findings on a photograph taken by a schoolboy showing the position of Kay Petre's car on the Byfleet Banking with Reg's MG bearing down on her, but nothing further was said on the matter, and for Reg Parnell racing came to a sudden end.

But it was not to end there. Reg had another try at the RAC, and at their 6 May 1938 meeting the Competitions Committee reported: 'Application for Return of Competition Licence: A letter from Mr R. Parnell asking if the Committee was prepared to indicate the period for which he was to be disqualified from holding a Competition licence was read. It was decided that in no circumstances would his licence be restored to him in 1938, but that the Committee was prepared to consider, without prejudice, an application from Mr Parnell to be granted a licence in 1939.'

The setback of not having a licence did not seem to dull Reg's enthusiasm for racing, and at the first meeting of 1938, the Coronation Trophy at Crystal Palace, he entered his MG with W. G. Everitt driving; he took sixth place with the car. Later in the season the MG was driven by A. F. Cuddon-Fletcher, and in only his second race with the car he won the BARC Campbell Circuit handicap event.

Reg then started to modify the car once more, as it was beginning to feel its age. He fitted independent front suspension from a Lancia Augusta, and Cudden-Fletcher had a number of good results throughout the season. At the same time the nose of the car was modified to give better cooling.

At the end of the season Cuddon-Fletcher decided to stop racing, and Reg sold the car to another former MG racer, Ian Nickols. Nickols kept the car, and indeed it was one of the racing cars that ran at the first post-war British race meeting at Gransden Lodge. The car was later sold to J. H. Webb, who was a prominent club racer in the 1950s, and it was to continue racing for many years. It is interesting that in his *Racing Car Reviews* Denis Jenkinson opined that '. . . strictly speaking it justifies being called a Parnell Special, as he carried out most of the modifications, which transformed it from the original well-known Magnette to the interesting vehicle it is today.'

As the 1938 season came to an end, and after Reg had written to the RAC yet again asking to have his licence back, they relented and at their Competitions Committee meeting on 28 September 1938 they reported: 'Application from a Competitor for the Removal of his Suspension: The Committee decided that the suspension of Mr R. Parnell should be terminated on the 31st December 1938, but any application from him for the issue of a Competition licence should be referred to the Committee before being dealt with.'

Reg received a letter to say that his licence would be returned to him in time for the 1939 racing season, and at the RAC Competitions Committee meeting of Wednesday 18 January 1939 it was reported: 'Issue of Competition Licence to a Competitor: The Committee agreed to the issue of an International Competition Licence to Mr R. Parnell. It was decided that promoters of races during the coming season in which Mr Parnell might compete should be asked to have his driving specially observed; a report in each case sent to the Committee for its consideration; and that Mr Parnell be informed that this action was being taken.'

(Racing enthusiasts might be interested to know that at that same meeting the following statement was made: 'Approval was given to the suggestion that a flag denoting to drivers the presence of oil on a track during the progress of a race should be recognised internationally. It was further suggested that the colour of the flag should be red and yellow in alternate stripes.' This became the oil flag recognised all over the world today.)

Having sold the MG, Reg purchased Dick Wilkins' BHW, a much modified version of a 5 litre Bugatti.

What must be remembered today is that in general terms Britain's motor racing fraternities played very much 'in their own sandpit', with Brooklands still dominating the scene as the home of British motor racing, rather as Silverstone does today. To a great extent the arrival of Donington in 1934 was to change that, but it appears that, to the Brooklands elite in the stockbroker belt around London, Donington could almost have been on another planet. Brooklands was also the home of the Special, and I feel that someday someone should write a truly detailed book about Brooklands Specials which, if nothing else, would demonstrate not only the ingenious but also the crackpot ideas of the British racing drivers of the day.

The BHW, despite being a Special that did not fit into any of the International racing classes of the day, was much more European and international in concept and looks than many of the other Specials. At that time, for instance, both the fastest and second fastest cars to have lapped Brooklands, the Cobb Napier-Railton Special and Bertram's Barnato-Hassan Bentley, were leviathans, whereas the BHW looked compact and had a remarkable similarity to the early 1934 Mercedes-Benz grand prix cars. It is also interesting that the man who design the BHW, Walter Hassan, had also designed the Barnato, so one could perhaps say that he designed horses for courses. The car had been commissioned by a well-known racing driver of the day, Richard (Dick) Wilkins, and the engine used was a straight-eight 4.9 litre Bugatti, hence the car's initials – B (Bugatti), H (Hassan) and W (Wilkins).

The engine came from a Bugatti Type 54 (chassis 54203), bought by Kaye Don in January 1932; it had been built to compete in grand prix racing, but within two years Mercedes-Benz and Auto Union had entered the fray and the car was uncompetitive against such opposition. It was an eight-cylinder unit with an 86 mm bore and 107 mm stroke, and twin overhead camshafts. It had been developed from the engine used in the Bugatti Type 50 sports cars at Le Mans in 1931. In that race the power of the engine and the inability of the tyres to stand up to the strain saw Maurice Rost crash heavily on the Mulsanne Straight, the driver being thrown out and badly injured. As a result of this, Jean Bugatti telephoned his father and on his advice withdrew the other two factory Type 50s.

Like the sports car before it, the Type 50 Bugatti grand prix car was heavy and did not handle particularly well. Even with drivers of the calibre of Marcel Lehoux, Count Czaykowski, Jean-Pierre Wimille and Kaye Don at the wheel, the cars did not perform well; indeed, Czaykowski was killed in his at Monza in 1933. Kaye Don's car was pressed into service at Brooklands, where he named it 'Tiger-Two', but on Brooklands the handling did not improve and one can imagine that it was something of a handful. So it was, around the end of 1937, that Wilkins bought the engine from Don to be put into his new car.

Walter Hassan's chassis offered independent front suspension, and at the rear used a pair of swing axles suspended on quarter elliptic rear springs. With an all-up weight of around 1 ton, it was not exactly a lightweight, and the balance between the rear suspension and the huge drum brakes did not help matters either when it came to handling. It certainly looked a good car, however, and during the 1938 season Dick Wilkins and A. P. Hamilton raced it at Brooklands before selling it to Reg Parnell.

Reg wanted to lighten the BHW and liner the engine down to

3 litres to make it suitable for Formula racing. In the opening meeting at Brooklands in March 1939 he ran it in the Second March Mountain handicap and finished third behind Jack Lemon Burton's Bugatti and Ian Connell's 4 litre Darracq. In the Third March Mountain Handicap (6 miles) he finished second behind Charles Mortimer's 2.3 Bugatti and ahead of Leslie Brooke's Riley.

It was touching that the first person who came up to congratulate him was Kay Petre. When asked about this, Reg said, 'Kay was grand about the whole thing. We are the best of friends and it was sporting of her to congratulate me today. It seemed to me to be the end of the world when I lost my racing licence. I know now I was a bit wild and all last year – 1938 – I watched the other drivers and realised that the faster and more successful they are the fewer risks they take. I studied their technique in the way they approached other drivers when overtaking and cornering. It has done me good and I can drive faster now without taking any risk.'

During that season Reg used the BHW for everything, as though to make up for his year away from racing. He ran it at Donington as well as in a number of hill-climb and sprint events. And buried deep amongst the Brooklands records is a note that Reg Parnell is the holder of the 'Manufacturers Circuit' lap record in the car.

Despite the fact that Reg was busily racing the BHW, he clearly saw in this car the idea of building a true grand prix car for the new formula that was expected to be announced for the 1941 season. Therefore, unaware that war would intervene, he started work on his own grand prix car, the Challenger, which was originally to be powered by a modified six-cylinder MG Magnette engine. Parnell was well used to this unit from his previous racing experience, but in the event it was never to power the car.

The Challenger had a tubular chassis designed by Parnell with independent front suspension and a de Dion rear axle, a layout that was to be standard practice in racing car design before and immediately after the war. Its original power unit was a Riley-based 1.5 litre (1,492 cc) supercharged ERA engine (perhaps borrowed from the R6B ERA that he had only recently bought). The whole car looked very much the part and, who knows, might have been a contender. But Hitler put paid to such hopes, and Reg only ran the Challenger at the Prescott hill-climb at the end of the season before storing it away for the duration.

At the end of the war he returned to the Challenger, which by now was without an engine. He installed a 1.5 litre Delage unit, which by that time was 18 years old. Although he himself never raced the car, his friend David Hampshire did, but any thoughts of developing the car further were left behind, and little is known of what actually happened to it. There were rumours that it had gone to America, but like many cars around that time it just disappeared and no doubt the Delage engine – well worth having – surfaced somewhere else. Who knows?

Chapter 3

1939-1947: The War –
Time To Speculate

WHEN WAR BROKE out Reg Parnell wanted to join the RAF and become a pilot, but he was told that he would be more useful if he stayed in Derby in the transport business, as the war effort would need people to run trucks and supplies all over Britain. As a result of this the Parnell family made a lot of money during the war, which was to be the basis of their future developments. This was reinforced by Reg's uncanny prescience to join forces with his friends the Ashmore brothers in the highly speculative venture of buying up all the racing cars that people wanted to sell because of the war.

As we have seen, Reg first met Joe and Fred Ashmore at the early Donington meetings, and they were to play a large part in his career thereafter, even though they were an unlikely pair. They came from a family of 'dealers', and after his early funfair experiences Fred was involved in the buying and selling of horses.

It is reckoned that Reg and the Ashmores had upwards of 32 racing cars and tons of spare parts salted away in barns and sheds during the wartime period. Around the time that war broke out people began to panic and fear for the future, so Reg and Joe Ashmore acquired as many cars and parts as they could find; they were to make a fortune from them after the war when everyone was desperate to find something to race. Parnell even bought the Bedford transporters used by ERA, converted them to ambulances and sold them to the Army.

It was once said that *one* of the racing cars he owned throughout the war was an ERA, when in fact he probably owned at least four ERAs during that period. For instance, he owned ERA R4A, the Pat Fairfield car, which had been bought by Norman Wilson in June 1937 after Fairfield had been killed in an accident. Then Norman Wilson himself was killed on active service in 1942, and the car was bought by Parnell and stored until March 1945, when he sold it to Bob Gerard.

David Weguelin in his superb book *The History of English Racing Automobiles Limited*, describes the negotiations as follows: 'News of an ERA for sale had reached the ears of F. R. (Bob) Gerard of Leicester, who had been a keen Riley enthusiast before the war, as well as a member of the ERA Club. Bob Gerard had worked through the war in his father's company, Parrs (Leicester) Ltd, a distributor of heavy commercial vehicles and diesel engines. His father promised him that when they achieved a certain level of turnover he could buy an ERA. Accompanied by his friend and colleague Frank Wooley, Gerard went to see Parnell and the car he was offering, which was R4A. It was lying in a shed with six racing machines, all of them in a dilapidated condition. R4A's dashboard was minus instruments and fitted with one that defied description, but they thought "it told French time in amps or something". When the bonnet was opened, dozens of screws and nuts fell to the floor, to reveal ". . .a miscellaneous collection of plugs, a couple of spanners, the remnant of a bird's nest and an old glove!". The car was also fitted with a crash gearbox. Around £1,000 changed hands and the car was taken back to Parrs' workshop where it was subjected to more industrial archaeology. It had evidently been in the hands of bodgers: joints were terrible; oil leaked everywhere; Whitworth nuts were forced on to BSF bolts, 3/8th in. bolts in 5/16th holes, etc.'

It was therefore decided that the only course was a complete strip-down and rebuild, yet despite this Gerard was able to have the car rebuilt by 14 July, and it ran in a Bristol MC hill-climb at Portishead on 11 August where Gerard was fastest car – but he was beaten for FTD by a 500 cc Triumph motor cycle!

Both Tim Parnell and Chris Ashmore admit that in the immediate post-war period, before their fathers founded Highfield Motors to concentrate on racing car preparation, the racing cars were often cobbled together by the mechanics in the transport business and were perhaps not as well prepared as they would have been by specialised racing mechanics.

Tim recalls: 'A lot of the cars Dad had were in a hell of a state and they arrived in boxes of bits and the lads who were working on the lorries were left to try and make something of them. Dad and Joe would buy anything and because people were worried that their places would be bombed and their cars destroyed they turned them willingly into cash. They were wheeler-dealers and there were a lot of them about during the war and they might even have contributed to bankrupting the country, but the war made a lot of people rich.

'Also my father was not averse to trying out the odd racing car on the roads during the war, and on one occasion he nearly cleaned up the local Lord of the Manor who happened to be out walking when Dad came flying round the corner in one of the Delages. Naturally the police came round to the transport business asking what was going on and what these racing cars were doing on the road when there was a war on. Dad also had one of those gas conversions done to his car, which became quite common as a way of conserving petrol. The trouble was that for most of the time it was just there for show, as dad was running on petrol from the lorry business.'

The first ERA Reg Parnell actually owned was R6B, which had originally been bought by Mrs Hall Smith for Robin Hanson to race. Hanson, however, gave up racing after the voiturette race at Rheims in 1939, and shortly afterwards Reg bought the car and decided to enter it for the Imperial Trophy race at Crystal Palace on 26 August of that year. Typically Reg built up his own 1,087 cc engine by both linering down then boring out the car's 1,500 cc unit. He finished fourth in his heat and fifth in the final, but any chance of developing the car evaporated just one week later on 3 September when war broke out. The car was taken back to Derby and dismantled; after the war it too went to Bob Gerard, ostensibly to be used as spares for R4A.

Another ERA that came into Reg's hands was R14B, the Johnny Wakefield car that appears to have been bought from Wakefield in 1941. The following year Wakefield was killed in action, and subsequently Parnell bought Wakefield's Maserati 4CL from the family and stored it. It was this car that was to be the one that Parnell initially used after the war. As regards R14B, there was an unsubstantiated story that the sound of a racing car was heard on the Donington circuit some time during the war, and the suspicion was that it was Reg with the ERA.

Even before the war ended there was mounting activity on the motor racing front, and Reg was in the thick of it. Towards the end of 1945 he bought ERA R8B/C, owned by Earl Howe, with a huge pile of spare parts including the Zoller supercharger on which Howe's mechanic had been working before the war. This car had a C-type chassis and, rebuilt with the Zoller supercharger, Reg took it to Turin for the race at Valentino Park on 1 September; however, he retired with supercharger trouble. Three weeks later the car was taken to Milan but again retired, this time with a broken back axle. It then appears to have been set aside in the garage until it was bought by Cuth Harrison in 1949 and subsequently raced by him for many years.

Probably the best buy that Reg made during the war was the Wakefield 4C 16-valve Maserati, which was one of only two imported into Britain in 1939. Wakefield has in some places been described as a member of the C. C. Wakefield family of Castrol fame, but in fact he was the son of a wealthy explosives manufacturer. He was certainly one of Britain's most promising racing drivers and, had the war not intervened, more would have been heard of him. As it was, he joined the Royal Navy's Fleet Air Arm but was killed when test flying a new plane. Reg bought the car from the Wakefield family. A touching postscript occurred in July 1946 when Reg travelled out to Albi for the Grand Prix there; the crowd stood for a minute's silence in memory of Wakefield, who had won the last Albi race in 1939. Reg also won the Jersey Road Race in the Wakefield Maserati in 1947.

Another 4C 16-valve Maserati was bought immediately after the war by Prince Bira, who raced it until the new 4CLT/48 Maserati arrived. In turn Reg was also to buy one of the new 4CLT/48 models; he sold his Wakefield car to Scotsman David Murray, who was later to found Ecurie Ecosse.

Such was the enthusiasm for motor sport after the war that on 22 April 1946 a speed trial was organised at Elstree, later to become the site of one of Britain's most famous film studios. Reg entered his new Maserati and finished third, but also ran a 2 litre Grand Prix Sunbeam in the event. He also entered his nephew Roy Parnell in a Delage made up of the many bits Reg had stored (of which more later). In the opinion of many contemporaries, Roy would have made a very successful racing driver had he wished to continue with the sport.

Three weeks later the Bugatti Owners' Club held their first post-war hill-climb at Prescott, and again Reg took part with the Maserati, clearly desperate to make up the time lost during five years of war.

But excitement was mounting elsewhere as an actual race meeting was being organised at Gransden Lodge by the enthusiastic Cambridge University Automobile Club. They actually had opposition from some people who thought that using a disused aerodrome was quite unsuitable. However, others in the sport praised the enthusiasts at Cambridge for rising to the occasion when the major established clubs had not. They used two runways and part of the perimeter road to make a 2.13-mile track. All the races were kept short, just three laps, with no handicaps and as many different classes as there were cars to fill them. There was even a scratch race organised for the fastest cars on the day. As if to set the tone of post-war British motor racing, the rain pelted down during practice, but it dried up somewhat during the day.

It was quite amazing how many cars had been resurrected, many of them pre-war racers. Ian Nickols turned up with Reg's old MG, and Alec Issigonis – later to become famous as the designer of the Mini – with his Lightweight Special. The 1,500 cc racing car event had a remarkably good entry with the three ERAs of Bob Gerard, Peter Whitehead and John Bainbridge, two Altas for George Abecassis and Charles Mortimer, and the Maseratis of Reg Parnell and David Hampshire. Roy Parnell was also entered in the Delage. In the race Reg had a battle with Bob Gerard, but Gerard spun and Reg went on to win. He also loaned his ex-Dixon Riley to Cuth Harrison who demolished the larger opposition.

Another competitor in the event was Dennis Poore, with the 3.8 litre Alfa Romeo that Reg had owned throughout the war. This famous car, which had been raced pre-war by Hans Reusch and Dick Seaman, had been bought by Robert Arbuthnot, who in turn sold it to Reg just prior to the war. Arbuthnot then bought it back from Reg, but was killed in a road accident on the Purley Way bypass in August 1946 driving his Peugeot.

Famous photographer and Brooklands driver Louis Klementaski was a close friend of Robert Arbuthnot: 'I received a telephone call from one of the members of the family asking whether I would go up to the Purley Bypass and photograph the wreck of the car. What had apparently happened was not Arbuthnot's fault. A Buick travelling in the opposite direction burst a tyre and the car swerved across the road into Arbuthnot's Peugeot and he was killed.

'Some time earlier Robert had been had up on the same Purley Bypass for speeding and on that occasion I went out with him and photographed this great big wide road as evidence in his defence, but I don't know if my pictures got him off or not.'

Robert Arbuthnot had earlier decided to compete in the first post-war Indianapolis 500 race. He had bought one of the two V12 Lagondas that had run at Le Mans in 1939 from Lord Waleran, who had shared the car in that race with Lord Selsdon. Arbuthnot took the normal body off the car and fitted an ugly lightweight body. The car was then taken to Indianapolis for the initial time trials, but it proved to be much too slow to qualify; it was later crashed in America, and the remains stayed there.

On Arbuthnot's death the family sold the Alfa Romeo to Dennis Poore, who became one of Britain's more successful drivers in Formule Libre racing with the car.

At the end of the Gransden Lodge meeting the six fastest finishers, including Reg, had a race-off from scratch. Abecassis took the lead in his 3.3 litre Bugatti followed by Wallington's 2.9 Alfa – the remaining half of the Austin Dobson Alfa Romeo Bimotore – and Monkhouse's 2.3 litre Bugatti. Reg was having trouble with the gear change from first to second, but he charged through the group to take the lead, only to suffer a blocked fuel line.

With his friends Leslie Brooke (ERA) and David Hampshire (Delage), Reg then made the long trip to the Spanish Border and the Albi circuit in the south of France. In some ways there was a touch of nostalgia, for as already mentioned Reg's Maserati 4CL was the car that Johnny Wakefield had used to win this very race in 1939. Obviously there was a lot of interest in the return of the car, but the scrutineers gave Reg a surprise when they told him that as he was British and it was an international event, he would have to repaint it in British Racing Green rather than Italian Racing Red! Reg protested and managed to persuade the organisers to buy the paint, and the job was done right there in the main street of Albi in front of everyone. The organisers had hoped for the Alfa Romeos, but they did not turn up; even the Milan Maseratis failed to arrive until after practice was over and had to start from the back of the grid.

The way the race was run was different from usual. True, there were two heats, but the aggregate time of each competitor over the two decided the winner. Reg ran second in the first race, and when Sommer retired with a failed supercharger Reg took the lead, followed by Louveau and Tazio Nuvolari. Nuvolari then took second, but Reg held him off until his magneto failed and he, too, was out. This same problem dogged him in the second heat, but he was still classified sixth.

It is generally accepted that although there were a number of motor race meetings held immediately after the war, the first true return of grand prix racing came on 21 July 1946 on a road circuit in Geneva. This was the Grand Prix des Nations, and 24 grand prix cars arrived for the event, which was remarkable as only a year earlier the war was still in progress. It was also a time for post-war reunions, and Louis Klementaski remembers the race well: 'It was the first time I had seen Reg Parnell since before the war and the first time I met his partners, Joe and Fred Ashmore. It was clear that they had made a packet out of the war, and they had not only stored all those racing cars but had been buying up Rolls-Royces and Bentleys for about £250 a time.'

The organisation of the race was not easy, and there were many arguments surrounding the event. Reg, Leslie Brooke and David

Hampshire actually travelled up from Albi without entries, hoping to get a run, and were accepted. Looking at Geneva today it is hard to believe that the start line was on the Avenue de France, and the course passed the old League of Nations Palace followed by a downhill to what was called Labour Monument Corner. It then ran along the Rue de Lausanne with its attendant tram lines (!) and on to the Quai Wilson before turning back to the Avenue de France. The lap was only 1.8 miles, so it was a tough course.

The field was led by Alfa Corse with four pre-war 158s to be driven by Farina, Trossi, Varzi and Wimille. Villoresi, Nuvolari and Sommer had Scuderia Milan's Maseratis, and there was quite a large British contingent including Raymond Mays, Ian Connell and Peter Whitehead.

Reg had clutch trouble in practice, but worked hard on the car to get it ready for the final session, ending up on the fourth row of the grid. He was able to show how competitive he was by running fifth on the opening lap before passing Prince Bira (ERA) into fourth. Wimille was well out in front with his Alfa and lapped Reg, but fourth place in this preliminary heat in such company was a good result.

The first six qualified for the final, so Reg was amongst them, starting on the third row. There was a an amusing incident just before the start when the diminutive Nuvolari was seen to take a rug, carefully fold it up and lay it under his seat so as to give him a better view of the track. Great friends and rivals, Nuvolari and Varzi were on the second row, and when Wimille jumped the start Nuvolari and Varzi went too. The starter, it is said, just shrugged his shoulders, put the flag under his arm and walked away.

Reg was in seventh place, but on the downhill to the Labour Monument Villoresi got it all wrong trying to outbrake Trossi's Alfa Romeo. He went up on the pavement, hit a lamp-post and ended up against some logs. Reg was right behind; he locked up and swerved all over the road but spun and stalled his engine in the middle of the corner. He tried to restart it but nothing happened, so he became the first retirement in the final.

It was around this time that Reg went down to Milan to try and persuade Alfa Romeo to sell him a 158, and there is a story that he was actually allowed to drive one, commenting that at 150 mph it sat on the road with the comfort of a touring car. But nothing came of it.

A year later, in 1947, Reg and Joe Ashmore were involved in another bizarre incident when they tried to buy one of the two pre-war 1.5 litre supercharged Mercedes Benz grand prix cars. Apparently Rudolph Carraciola, the former Mercedes team driver, was living in

Zurich and had both cars with him; they had been smuggled into Switzerland before the war ended. He had refused requests to race or sell them, but the post-war Economic Welfare Department seized them and put them up for sale at £10,000 each. Always with their fingers on the pulse, Reg and Joe, with long-time friend Rob Walker, realised that one had been sent to Indianapolis in 1946 for Carraciola to drive, but that the other was still for sale.

Chris Ashmore remembers the occasion because his father had drawn the £10,000 necessary to buy the car, but there was a problem. Despite the fact that the Swiss and the British Control Commission agreed to the deal taking place, the Americans objected, saying that they would not like to see German racing cars running so soon after the war. This did not seem to worry the Italians, as they just wheeled out their cars and got on with it. However, the whole deal was stopped. When asked about it, Reg said that he wanted the car in Britain in order to take it apart and learn from it so that Britain could build a successful grand prix car. He also added that he had two British manufacturers who had assured him of their interest in the project.

Over in Northern Ireland the Ulster Automobile Club took advantage of their different laws to run a road race for the Ulster Trophy on a course outside Belfast. Just about everyone who had a racing car was desperate to go and race on a true British road race circuit, and they were led by Reg Parnell. However, he suffered loss of oil pressure when warming up the car and practised in a borrowed one. He managed to get the Maserati repaired for the race, but the slow gear change from first to second allowed Prince Bira to get past.

Bob Gerard also enjoyed a tremendous start. Reg had told his pit crew not to give him any signals, but the pace between Bira, Gerard and Parnell was such that Reg went flat out, broke the lap record, then started waving his arms at the pit crew to tell them to give him signals as to where he stood in the race. A lap later the pit board was put out, complete with various arm gestures from the crew advising him to put his foot down. Both Bira and Reg passed Gerard, then had one of those racing battles that everyone remembers. They kept breaking the lap record, and as they passed the pits to start the last lap they were only a car's length apart. Reg tried everything to get past, and both drivers were risking their engines. Finally Reg tried a move on one of the corners, the Maserati slewed and the race went to Bira.

Chapter 4

1947-1948: ERAs, Maseratis and the Italian Connection

IN 1946 THE opportunity had arisen for Reg Parnell to buy the original ERA, R1A, which at the time was owned by H. W. Motors, the John Heath/George Abecassis company, and it was this car that Reg took to Sweden for the two winter grand prix races. These remarkable ice races took place in February 1947, when Sweden mostly 'basks' in temperatures hovering around −15°. Indeed, some 30 years later I went to a Swedish ice race on a frozen lake and saw drivers trying to start a Fiat Abarth by warming up the carburettors with a blow torch! One can imagine what it must have been like trying to start an ERA. Reg took the car first to Rommehed and won his first major race, his first grand prix. He then moved to the meeting at Vallentuna Lake and won again.

These ice races brought Reg Parnell and Wilkie Wilkinson together again. At the time Wilkinson was out of work. The war had seen the closure of Bellevue Garage, Wilkie's wartime job with Rotol had come to an end, and he was looking for a job back in motor racing. As he tells it in his biography *Wilkie*, he received a letter from Humphrey Cook, Chairman of ERA Limited, asking him to come for a chat with the possible offer of a job as test driver and team manager for a new post-war ERA team. When he arrived he found the small company paralysed by a power cut and amid much embarrassment Cook could only offer a 'don't ring us, we'll ring you' arrangement, as he still had to get things re-organised.

As Wilkie walked out of the door he heard a familiar voice cry out. 'Hello, Wilkie, what are you doing here ?'

It was Reg in a desperate hurry to find spare parts for his ERA, which had blown an engine in Sweden during the ice races. Reg asked Wilkie to wait while he got his spares, and when he returned to the car with a big box of bits he asked Wilkie if he was prepared to fly to Sweden right away with these spares and get the ERA running again. As Wilkie remarked, 'Knowing Reg of old – he was a very shrewd operator – I asked what he intended to pay me. True to form, he asked me what I wanted. It was not a long job, so I said £20 plus all expenses. "You're on," said Reg with a big smile, and handed me the box of spares. It contained con-rods, valves, valve springs, pushrods, gaskets, bearings, cam-followers – everything one could think of. Reg said it must travel to Sweden as my luggage as there was no time to get export or import licences.'

Two days later and one week before the second Swedish race, Wilkie flew to Gothenburg and picked up the open Jeep that Reg had left parked there. The last vehicle anyone would want to drive in Sweden in February is an open Jeep with no heater, particularly when he had to drive to Stockholm, a formidable journey even today. The ERA was parked in the garage of the hotel and Wilkie found a hole in the side of the crankcase big enough for him to put his hand in and feel around for the damage! It took him a week to repair.

The race that weekend was on Vallentuna Lake north of Stockholm, where a 3½-mile circuit had been snowploughed. The surface was sheet ice, and as nobody was allowed to use studded tyres the organisers spread gravel over the entire course then sprayed it with water to provide a sandpaper-like finish.

At the previous race Reg, his pal Leslie Brooke and George Abecassis had virtually had it all their own way, as the ship bringing all the French drivers had been frozen up in the ice somewhere in the Kattegat; but now all the Frenchmen had arrived. After practice Reg was discussing road-holding with his companions when he suddenly realised that back home he had some extra-long hubs to enable the fitting of twin rear wheels for hill climbs. He therefore phoned his nephew Roy and told him to get the hubs and a spare set of wheels to London Airport and over to Gothenburg that night.

They duly arrived and were put on to the car, and when Reg went out to practice with twin rear wheels all hell was let loose. Raymond Sommer complained to the organisers, but Parnell had checked the regulations and the organisers agreed with him that there was nothing to say that twin rear wheels could not be used, so Reg was not only allowed to run them but also won against all the French opposition. Parnell's prize money was considerable, so they had a real party led by Leslie Brooke.

'Brookie' had won the George Cross during the war for rescuing people from bombed buildings during the Coventry raids; he had no fear, and a bizarre concept of what made a good party. Back at the hotel after the race, Reg and the Ashmores heard a noise at the window and looked out to see Leslie Brooke on the window ledge – they were three storeys up! Brookie had climbed out of the window of his room next door and had walked along a narrow ice-covered ledge to peer into Reg's window. Nobody dared open the window in case they swept him off the ledge, and he eventually crawled back to his own room only to fall on to the wash basin and destroy it.

Their exploits were not overlooked by the Swedish press. The local Stockholm newspaper *Idrottsbladet* reported that '. . .the English were jolly fellows – it seemed as if the three drivers, Parnell, Brooke and Abecassis, were much more tough than the French with the exception of Chaboud. They didn't seem to care about the cold weather. Above all Brooke was a funny chap and his orders for more champagne at both Borlange and Rosenblad after the Vallentuna race will be fresh in our minds for a long time.'

Lest you get the idea that Reg and Brooke were no more than pranksters, they both took it upon themselves to go to London and meet up with Sir Stafford Cripps, President of the Board of Trade in the post-war socialist Attlee Government, to underline to him the importance of motor racing. They pointed out from their experiences on the Continent that spectators all over Europe were enthralled by motor racing and it was good for the country. The popular image of Cripps at that time was a skull-like face and an absence of any sense of humour or compassion. However, after he had received the Parnell/Brooke treatment his attitude was entirely favourable, and it was reported that he was sympathetically disposed towards the concept of financial sponsorship by the Government for a full-scale bid for international racing honours. However, it remained just that, a concept, swept under the carpet of the social changes that the Government was to make in Britain and that were to throw a blanket of austerity over the country for many years to come.

Reg only ran R1A on one other occasion, at a MMES speed trial on a course at Cofton Hackett just south of Birmingham, where he set up Fastest Time of the Day. Joe Ashmore shared the driving of the car and finished second fastest. Joe was also entered for the Jersey Road Race of 1947 with the same car before his brother Fred took it over and raced it until the end of the season. It was then sold to another of Reg's pals, David Hampshire, whose family pharmaceutical business made Zubes cough tablets of 'Zubes for your Tubes!' fame. Four years later the car was sold to two young Scottish drivers, Ron Flockhart and Alastair Birrell, who in 1952 formed a team called Alba Union –

Alba being a former name of Scotland. Later that year Flockhart's career took off when he bought the ex-Raymond Mays R4D ERA.

Early in 1947 *Motor* magazine road-tested Reg's ex-Wakefield 4CL Maserati on what was termed 'a deserted aerodrome near Donington'. This turned out to be the site of the present-day East Midlands Airport, which had been used by Reg on a number of occasions for private testing.

With the war over Reg and the Ashmores decided to form a garage business to run the racing car, so Highfield Garages (Derby) Ltd was founded with an authorised share capital of £20,000 in £1 shares. The Directors and principal shareholders were Reg, Joe and Fred Ashmore, but following the Swedish races Reg offered Wilkie Wilkinson a job as works manager, which he accepted even though at about the same time he had received an invitation to join Goldie Gardner, who wanted him to be chief mechanic on his various record-breaking exploits. Wilkie comments in his autobiography that he was offered 500 free shares in the Parnell company if he accepted the job; that was in March 1947, and he was not given the shares or made a Director until 17 November.

During 1947 Reg bought the first of the E-type ERAs (GP1); it had been campaigned by Peter Whitehead since 1946, but he had experienced nothing but trouble with the car, ending with it retiring from the 1947 Jersey Road Race with a split fuel tank. Reg had been on hand and had offered to buy the car. This was not the first time that he had been involved with GP1, as he had stored it throughout the war even though he did not actually own it. It was duly entered for the Grand Prix de La Marne at Reims.

In practice the supercharger seized, shearing the drive. Wilkie and George Boyle of ERA stripped down the blower to find some of the blades bent. The drive could not be repaired and Reg was desperate to collect his starting money, so they took the innards out of the supercharger and replaced the carburettors; according to Wilkie it became the first ERA ever to race unsupercharged. After a few laps Parnell added a touch of showbusiness and came into the pits shouting loudly that the engine had lost power! Wilkie made an attempt at repairs and sent Reg out again for another few slow laps before he came back in and retired with engine trouble! Ironically sister car GP2 was running in the same race with Leslie Brooke, but it too retired, this time with a broken gearbox.

One race Reg missed was at the Commignes circuit near Toulouse on the Mediterranean. However, he loaned his 4CL Maserati to Joe Ashmore to drive – something he was always reluctant to do – while

Fred ran the older ERA. Chris Ashmore remembered the occasion well: 'Dad was hit from behind in the race and the car turned over and he landed up in hospital – the Maserati was written off. My uncle Fred put the ERA into the river, then got upset because he had lost his cigarette lighter and one of his shoes, so he went off to a pub to have a drink.' Joe Ashmore retired from racing after this crash.

Reg's flirtation with GP1 did not last long. The car broke its de Dion tube at the Ulster Trophy in Ireland where it had briefly led. It was then entered for the French Grand Prix held at the pre-war Lyons–Parilly circuit. He also entered the E-type ERA with Wilkie Wilkinson as reserve driver, and it proved not only to be an eventful race but also the last straw as far as the temperamental GP1 was concerned. In the early stages of the race Reg just could not get to grips with the car and called into the pits to say that the handling was all wrong and perhaps the de Dion tube was acting up again. Wilkie had a look and everything seemed to be fine, but a few laps later Reg was back again, still not happy. He told Wilkie to take the car out, so off went the chief mechanic, still not sure of the circuit but driving as fast as he could.

After 13 laps he arrived at a corner to find that he had no steering – the badly welded pin had sheared. The car ploughed off the road, mounted the grass verge and eventually stopped. Reg and Leslie Brooke rushed up to find out what had happened, because the crash had taken place on the straight just before the corner. Wilkie reached over to the steering wheel and spun it round and round. Reg's only comment was that he might have been driving! He never raced the car again, and two months later it appeared at the Lausanne Grand Prix with David Hampshire at the wheel; it retired again.

Much is talked about starting money, the life blood of motor racing in those days. Although the amounts do not appear much by today's standards, 50 years ago they represented a lot of money, particularly at a time when the British Government only allowed British citizens to take £25 (perhaps the equivalent of about £500 today) out of the country in any given year. For the record, and bearing in mind the above comparison of values, Reg Parnell's starting money for 1947 included £200 for the Albi Grand Prix, £130 for Geneva, £250 for Turin, £225 for Milan and £250 for the Penya Rhin in Spain. Add to this any prize money and oil and petrol bonuses, and it can be seen that it was possible to make a reasonable living from motor racing.

Then there was Reg's connection with Scuderia Ambrosiana, the well-known Italian racing team. This had been founded in November 1936 as the Scuderia Automobilistica Ambrosiana by four of Italy's up and coming gentlemen racing drivers led by Count Giovanni (Johnny) Lurani (in the original team he was 'Giannino' or 'Little Johnny'). His three partners were the legendary Franco Cortese, Luigi 'Gigi' Villoresi and Eugenio Minetti. They all owned their own cars but worked as a team and were very successful up to and immediately after the war. Cortese, who won the Targa Florio in a Frazer Nash, and Villoresi, who had many victories with his Maserati 4CL, were their most successful drivers. They also entered the young Alberto Ascari in some races in 1948.

In 1949 Ovidio Capelli became President of Scuderia Ambrosiana and a few more gentlemen drivers came with him, including Eraldo Nicosia, Corrado Manfredini and the three brothers Dore, Carlo and Massimo Leto di Priolo. In the ten years from 1955 to 1965 they competed mainly in Italian events with touring and GT cars, as well as rallies, but then the team was wound up. In the 1990s friends and some of the sons of the members re-activated the club and occasionally took part in historic events; by now Massimo Leto di Priolo was President, assisted by his son-in-law Giovanni Iachino. At the Intereuropa Cup historic meeting at Monza in 1993 I was invited to a private party at which Count Lurani and Massimo Leto di Priolo were hosts, and there was talk of them producing a detailed history of the Scuderia, but nothing so far has come of it.

The link between Reg and the team remains something of a mystery, except perhaps to those of us who were conscious of what was going on around that time. There is no doubt that the association was to their mutual advantage. Equally there is no doubt that it facilitated many transactions that, due to exchange control laws at the time, could not otherwise have taken place. For instance, when Reg bought a brand new 4CLT/48 Maserati from the factory in 1948, it was impossible that the purchase could be covered by the British Government's £25 per year allowance. It appears that Scuderia Ambrosiana and Reg operated a system whereby money and cars changed hands by a mysterious system of barter and subterfuge, and this continued later with Reg's dealings with Enzo Ferrari. There was one story that the reason why the team was called Scuderia Ambrosiana was because they had Banco Ambrosiana – the Vatican Bank – behind them, and due to its unique position as the bank of the Roman Catholic Church worldwide it was allowed to trade freely across international exchange control barriers. However, this was not the case. The team was called Ambrosiana simply because the patron Saint of Milan, where it was founded, was St Ambrose. (During the 1950s the man who was to become Ferrari team manager, Eugenio

Dragoni, founded his own motor racing team called Scuderia St Ambroeus for the same reason.)

Another story I was told, which sounded a bit more plausible, was that there was a standing arrangement between Reg and Count Lurani whereby Reg would pay for some of the expenses that the Ambrosiana drivers incurred when they raced in Britain in return for Ambrosiana paying an equal sum of Reg's expenses on the Continent, so saving valuable currency in exchange control.

However, there were also other methods. Chris Ashmore remembers the occasion when his father Joe bought his 4CLT/48 Maserati (chassis No 1593, which had been Ascari's factory car) on 24 February 1949; the money was paid to an Italian ice-cream man in London, who presumably had a way of getting it to Italy! Reg's own 4CLT (chassis No 1596, a brand new car) had been bought on 14 September 1948. Both Chris and Tim Parnell are convinced that around a year later there was a tremendous row between Reg and Count Lurani when one of the cars went back to Italy on a triptyque, but never returned. (According to Maserati records a 4/CLT, chassis No 1596, was obtained by Scuderia Ambrosiana on 13 November 1949!)

Certainly Reg and Scuderia Ambrosiana enjoyed a productive friendship and partnership until it gradually petered out as the years went by and exchange control became easier.

There was a final Scuderia Ambrosiana link when, in March 1957, a dinner was held in the Midland Hotel, Derby, to mark Reg's retirement from motor racing. It was organised by some of his motor racing pals including John Green, John Dalton and David Hampshire, and there were many letters and telegrams, including one from Dore Leto di Priolo on behalf of Scuderia Ambrosiana, which read as follows.

To our dear friend Reginald Parnell,

It is a great pity that our Count Lurani, Mr Minetti or myself are unable to be with you to share your most intimate emotions. We will never forget for one moment the man to whom Scuderia Ambrosiana is indebted for so many successes. You were only concerned with sport and gallantry and your retirement is regretted by everybody who met you and appreciated you in your field. You always gave most generously as a racing pilot and you well deserve satisfactions from life. We look forward to meeting you again soon when we can go over and over all the nice times we had together.

Remaining for very long, your best friends and admirers. Let me shake hands once more with you today in spirit on behalf of all your Italian followers.

Dore Leto di Priolio
Scuderia Ambrosiana, Milano

Internationally speaking the 1948 motor racing season in Europe was the first indication that racing was returning to normal. There were more and bigger race meetings, and the pattern of events that had existed before the war was beginning to take shape again. The greatest change, however, was in Britain, where the whole motor racing scene was transformed. Replacing the elitist and quaint races and formulae that had characterised Brooklands were races for everything on new circuits made from old airstrips, the most notable of which was Silverstone, where the British Grand Prix was held.

The drivers that straddled the wartime gap were keen to get back to the sport after a long lapse, while other new boys were waiting in the wings thanks to the wider interest in and democratisation of motor racing. In the immediate post-war period nobody cared about who you were – if you had a car you could race, and whatever the car was it could be accommodated. Never was the French term 'Formula Libre' (Free Formula) treated more liberally than in those days. In a sense Reg was in his element as he had a number of cars and had also sold cars to friends, so it was time to spread his wings.

During the winter Reg had been persuaded by his friend Cuth Harrison to be his passenger in the Sheffield and Hallamshire Trophy Trial. The car was a Harford Special and on the muddy and slippery hillsides Reg's weight and bouncing no doubt helped the pair to a win in the event. Reg was also involved in a local campaign to bring Donington back as a motor racing circuit. It was still owned by the War Office and the 'Give Us Donington' campaign was launched at a luncheon where Reg said that he believed the War Office was in a position to return the circuit to private hands, and that the local Donington Parish Council had offered their support. He then donated £50 to get the campaign started, but it was to be many years before local builder Tom Wheatcroft came along and made this dream a reality.

By now Reg was being recognised as one of Britain's best racing drivers, and in turn his driving style had changed. Gone were the wild days of old. Indeed, former Polish refugee and later mechanic to Stirling Moss, Alf Francis, commented on Reg's driving on one of the first occasions he saw him race, the British Empire Trophy in the Isle of Man in 1948.

'The thing that impressed me most was the magnificent driving of Reg Parnell in the Maserati, particularly the way he cut past the pits. Every lap his wheels were within an inch of the low wall on which we were standing, and it was amazing to me how they passed repeatedly over exactly the same spot. Those of us who stood on the wall to give signals had to be very careful, and anyone who sat down and dangled his legs over the wall was running the risk of losing them. Parnell drove a wonderful race. He was the only man who looked to my inexperienced eye like a potential champion. His handling of the Maserati seemed head and shoulders above the other drivers and I could not see his equal in that race. I would say he was the Stirling Moss of his day, although admittedly the Maserati was a hard car to beat. His magnificent drive should have been rewarded with victory, but fate stepped in on the last lap as the chequered flag was unfurled. The Maserati ran out of fuel and the auxiliary fuel tank feed failed due, I believe, to there being no air supply to the tank. As soon as the news came over the loudspeakers we all shouted to Parnell's mechanics, "Take some petrol out to him." They did so, being told by all and sundry to get a move on, but it was not possible to get the Maserati going and the ERA of Geoff Ansell took the chequered flag.'

Reg became one of the small group of privateer racing drivers who toured the Continent with his car. It gave him tremendous experience racing against the likes of Nuvolari, Villoresi and Farina.

On 29 April 1948 the bedevilled E-type ERA GP1 was dragged out again for the Jersey Road Race with Fred Ashmore in the driving seat. However, the car had fuel feed trouble and retired yet again. A fortnight later Reg decided to have another go and entered for the Monaco Grand Prix, but this time GP1 retired with a broken piston. Finally, two weeks later he offered it to Wilkie Wilkinson for the British Empire Trophy race in the Isle of Man, but the engine blew up. The car was taken back to Derby and put in the back of the shop until Peter Whitehead and Peter Walker came along and bought it back for the 1949 racing season.

Reg's flirtation with ERAs continued when he bought R11B from E. G. Pool. This car had been raced by Robert Cowell and Gordon Watson during the 1946 season. Around that time Cowell had a much publicised sex-change and became Roberta Cowell. It was one of the first sex change operations undertaken on a Briton, and was performed in Sweden. He, or now she, came back to a barrage of sensational journalistic coverage.

The ERA had been sold to Pool having been badly damaged in an accident, and he apparently never raced it, so Reg stepped in and bought it. Having seen the success Bob Gerard was having with his 2 litre ERA, Reg made up a 2 litre engine and put it in the car, but only used it for hill climbs, running at Shelsey Walsh that year, then taking it to Bo'ness in Scotland where he shared it with Sheila Derbyshire. He also ran the car at Bouley Bay hill climb in Jersey before returning to Britain and selling it to the great enthusiast Peter Bell. Bell entered former *Autosport* technical editor and racing driver John Bolster in the car, but he had a heavy accident in the British Grand Prix, which ended his racing career. Subsequently the car was raced and hill climbed by Ken Wharton, again thanks to Peter Bell.

The other ERA that Reg bought but never raced was R2A, which George Abecassis had owned. Indeed, it is only credited with one race while in Reg's hands, the Dutch Grand Prix at Zandvoort when Fred Ashmore finished fifth. It was then sold on to George Nixon who continued to race it.

Over the years Reg owned more of the small number of ERAs ever built than anyone else save the factory itself – seven, at my count. For the record Reg once drove the famous 2 litre Mays car R4D at a minor race meeting at Gamston in August 1951, and won the race with it.

In case it might be thought that Reg and Joe were sharper than everyone, there was one occasion when they were taken in by the great Freddie Dixon. Dixon offered them both his own and the Percy McLure Rileys. The Derby duo managed to hammer the price down a bit and happily set off with the cars only to find when they tested them that they were not very quick.

Joe Ashmore rang Dixon to complain, to which Freddie replied, 'You nicked the cars from me at that price – now you have to pay for the camshafts!' Apparently Dixon had removed the hot cams, then sold them to Parnell and Ashmore for close to the same price that they had paid for the cars!

One of the most fascinating cars owned by Reg at that time was the 'Chula Delage'. Its background history is complicated, and I am grateful for information supplied by John Stonebreaker in his article 'The Black Delage' (*Automobile Quarterly*, Vol 30 No 2).

We must go back to 1929 and the occasion when the Monegasque Louis Chiron entered a Delage for the Indianapolis 500 race. It was believed to be the car that Robert Benoist had raced successfully during the 1927 season, and although Chiron had acquired the car and entered it privately, Louis Delage claimed that he was still the owner.

Chiron took the car to seventh place at Indianapolis, then returned to Europe where he sold it to Robert Senechal, who raced it in the 1930 and '31 French Grands Prix. After an accident, Earl Howe was able to buy it from Senechal and brought it to England. He already owned a similar Delage that had been sold to him by land speed record-holder Malcolm Campbell. The latter was badly damaged in a crash at Monza, so Howe switched to his other Delage for the rest of the season. (Part of the mystery about these Delages is that it appears few people knew that Howe actually had two of them, his deal with Senechal having been kept very quiet.) Many years later, in the 1960s, Chiron wrote to Delage expert Alan Burnard admitting that his Indianapolis car and the one that later became known as the Seaman Delage were one and the same. This is the same chassis later owned by Rob Walker (Car No 4, Chassis No 18488).

When Earl Howe therefore sold his Delage to Dick Seaman he sold him the Chiron-Senechal car along with the rest of the parts left from the Malcolm Campbell car. In turn this car was modified by Giulio Ramponi and with it Seaman literally blossomed as a top-rank racing driver. Ramponi had produced the most powerful and successful Delage of the time, and it gave Seaman many victories in 1936. Subsequently he was invited to join Mercedes-Benz, and sold his Delage and all the parts to Prince Chula of Siam for his cousin, Prince Bira, to drive.

Chula had two new chassis produced with independent front suspension; some of the parts from the Seaman car were put into this new one and it was called the 'Chula Delage'. To complicate matters further, Chula bought another Delage. However, Bira was never at home with the car and spent more time racing his ERA 'Remus', so by the end of the war the 'Chula Delage' and all the spare parts arrived at Reg Parnell's door. Sorting through everything, Reg not only built up the second independent suspension chassis but also rebuilt the Seaman chassis, so with the 'Chula' car he now had three Delages!

Reg's good friend David Hampshire bought the 'Chula Delage' and the Seaman car and raced one of them at the Geneva Grand Prix in 1947. Meanwhile Rob Walker bought the third chassis, engine and other major parts, which were linked to the Chiron-Senechal-Howe and Seaman car(s), a fact proved by the oak blocks that Ramponi had put between the dumb irons. That car was lovingly rebuilt for Walker by John Chisman, but in 1968 it was destroyed, save for a few parts, in a fire at Walker's Garage in Dorking, Surrey. John Chisman went to work again and with the aid of Delage enthusiasts rebuilt the car once more.

Meanwhile the 'Chula Delage' was sold to Eckart Berg in Germany along with some of the parts of the Seaman car, so like the woodman's axe the components of these various Delages were swopped around, aided and abetted by the diligence and enthusiasm of Reg Parnell.

Chapter 5

1948-1950:
The Wider Stage

REG PARNELL'S 1948 season began with the Jersey Road Race on the St Helier Circuit. There was quite a good entry for the event, mostly British, but the star was Luigi Villoresi with a 4CL. Unfortunately he had gearbox trouble on the starting line and lost a lap. When he got going he only ran six laps before the gearbox seized again. Reg, still driving his old 4CL, led on the opening lap but was passed by Prince Bira's similar 4CL. This threw a tyre tread and Reg went back into the lead, only to be passed by Bob Gerard in his ERA. Reg's car was not running well, and after changing wheels he ran third behind George Abecassis in an old 6C Maserati, Gerard taking first.

One of the most interesting races of that year's season was the Dutch Grand Prix, held at the new circuit of Zandvoort in Holland. This circuit was laid out on sand-dunes and was operated by John Hugenholtz, who was later to become a prominent circuit designer (one of his best-known projects is the Suzuka circuit in Japan where the present Japanese Grand Prix takes place). Hugenholtz is often quoted as being the designer of Zandvoort, but this is one circuit that he did not design. Indeed, the outline of the circuit had been planned by the burghers of Zandvoort before the Second World War. There is a story that during the war, when Holland was occupied by the Germans, the German artillery commandant spoke with the mayor of Zandvoort about building gun emplacements along the coast to bombard England. The mayor, knowing about the circuit plan, allegedly persuaded the Germans to place their guns in a particular area, then gave them a sketch of the roadways they would have to construct to service the guns; these of course coincided with the shape of the circuit. It may not be a true story, but I find it intriguing – and heart-warming!

Although they now had a circuit, the Dutch did not have the organisational skills to run a motor race meeting. They therefore contacted the British Racing Drivers Club and asked them to stage the meeting, which was a great success.

All the gang then went to the BRDC Empire Trophy race on the Isle of Man, which was very much a British affair even though it was an International event. Again Reg went ahead, and by half distance he had a lead of nearly a full lap. He had decided to go without a fuel stop and had added an extra fuel tank to his car, but when he switched over to the reserve tank half way round the last lap nothing happened, the engine started to splutter and the car stopped. Reg had to stand beside his car, half a lap to go and over a lap in the lead, and watch Geoffrey Ansell drive past with his Maserati 4CL to win the event.

In September Reg made the long trip to the Italian Grand Prix, which that year was run on the circuit in Valentino Park beside the river in Turin. This is a picturesque circuit and the race took place on the wide roads within the park. To this day there is still a reminder of racing there as the city fathers have permanently marked the three-sided box on the road surface where Alberto Ascari started his last race on the circuit.

A very young Tim Parnell was taken to this race by his father and he remembers that it was on this occasion that Ferrari used Vandervell Thin Wall bearings in its cars for the first time. Later Reg was never to go abroad without a car-load of Thin Wall bearings, which he sold to foreign racing drivers desperate to use them in their engines.

One of the reasons why Reg was able to race in Turin was that he had gone out to Modena to meet with Adolfo Orsi and his son Omer to take delivery of one of the brand new 4CLT/48 Maserati grand prix cars. The race was also significant in that it was the first in which the 1.5 litre Ferraris raced – with Sommer, Farina and Bira driving. Around the same time Bira had bought another of these new Maseratis. For Reg it was a good trip, as he finished fifth.

On 2 October the RAC organised the British Grand Prix for the first time at Silverstone. The present-day motor racing enthusiast might not recognise much of the track as it was then. The start line was in the section after Abbey Curve and before Woodcote, and the layout used the central runways, forming an 'X' shape in the middle. Contemporary photographs of the start show racing cars pointing in all directions and covered in mechanics – Leslie Johnson's E type ERA, Cuth Harrison's ERA, and Reg's spanking new Maserati standing on the front row of the grid with nobody around it.

The crowd for that first Grand Prix at Silverstone was estimated at

130,000, which, when related to the primitive or indeed non-existent facilities that existed at the time, was quite remarkable, and came close to a football international at Hampden Park, Glasgow, for the largest single crowd for a British sporting event. It was the first RAC-run British Grand Prix since the Brooklands event of 1927, and the first grand prix in England since Donington in 1938.

All the leading teams were present, so here was a chance for the British drivers, many of them in pre-war cars, to see how they compared with the foreign opposition. However, there was an odd situation for Villoresi and Ascari, as they had arrived too late for practice and their factory Maseratis had to start from the back of the grid. The fact that they took the lead in the race after just three laps shows the gulf that existed between the professional factory cars and the private owners. The two Italians swopped places, refuelled and changed wheels, yet it was Villoresi who ended up an easy winner. Baron De Graffenried, in his older 4CL Maserati, had led originally, and Silverstone was to become one of his favourite circuits. Bob Gerard finished third. Reg was out of luck, retiring on the first lap with a leaking fuel tank; he had spun and hit one of the landing lights that were still embedded at the edge of the runway, which split the tank.

A trip to Italy for the Italian Grand Prix proved to be a disaster. Reg qualified last on the grid, 5 seconds slower than Cuth Harrison's aged ERA. Throughout the race the car ran on three cylinders, so it was no surprise when Reg retired on lap 17 with engine trouble.

When Bira bought his 4CLT Maserati he sold his previous 4CL to an up and coming English driver with an Italian name, Roy Salvadori. Roy's parents had come to Dovercourt, Essex, from Italy many years before the war, and Roy had taken up motor racing with various cars including an MG and an ex-Nuvolari Alfa Romeo. The 4CL was much more modern than the Alfa, so he started to deal with Reg.

'Reg was very helpful with bits that he would either loan me or sell me. They were not exactly new bits, you understand, but at least they used to get you out of a hole. He was the top British driver and had more experience with Maseratis than anyone else in England. I found him easy to talk to and become friendly with as long as you played the game. If you did that he played the game with you. Reg had a good reputation and was basically honest. You must remember that back in those days when you bought racing cars you were very much in injury time. I felt even then Reg tried to do too much and I wouldn't have liked to have driven a car prepared by Reg because he was preparing far too many cars and couldn't give the attention needed to the number of cars he was preparing.

'As a driver I think Reg was always underestimated. He had a very light touch with a car, was particularly good in the wet and was a contender. Give Reg a poor car and he would adapt himself to it. Reg would make it work and later on, when I shared a car with him, I never had any trouble even though he had set it up. I found it was always a pretty good mix.'

In 1949 Reg moved on to a wider international stage, entering the Buenos Aires Grand Prix in Argentina. One of the other drivers was 41-year-old Jean-Pierre Wimille in one of Amédée Gordini's little Simca Gordinis. Wimille, who normally raced with a canvas helmet and goggles, approached Reg after he had finished his practice laps and asked to borrow his crash helmet. It is alleged that Wimille remarked, 'I hope I don't have to use it.' A few moments later he was dead, killed in a mysterious accident. One theory was that he had crashed trying to avoid a woman who had run across the track in front of him. Whatever the reason, the little blue Gordini hit a tree and Wimille suffered a fractured skull and crushed throat. Today he is remembered by few people, but he had been very successful with Alfa Romeo grand prix cars, and it is said that he was the model on which Juan Manuel Fangio based his driving style.

In one of the two races held in Argentina Reg finished second in pouring rain, and the local commentator explained to the crowd that it was only right for an Englishman to finish well up as it always rained in England. However, as we were to see on many occasions, Reg was blindingly fast in the wet.

During 1949 Wilkie Wilkinson began to give second thoughts to his career at Highfield; he was tired of working on a variety of racing cars and driving for long hours on the Continent, and in February he had collapsed from overwork. A new Highfield customer was a middle-aged Scots accountant called David Murray, who had bought the ex-Wakefield 4CL Maserati from Reg and was later to buy the 4CLT and an ex-Scuderia Ambrosiana Formula 2 Ferrari. Murray was shrewd and had gained a good idea of how motor racing worked at that time and how, perhaps, he had been taken advantage of in his ignorance. He was impressed by Wilkie's work and broached the idea that he should take his cars away from the Parnell stable and set up a garage business in Edinburgh to prepare not only his but other people's sports and luxury cars with Wilkie at the helm. Wilkie agreed and sold his shares in Highfield Garage to Reg; Reg agreed to split the Maserati spares between him and David Murray.

As Wilkie remarks in his autobiography, 'I was able to warn David that the split, as carried out by Reg, gave Reg all the best parts, despite

Reg's insistence that both piles were of equal value. We did a swop in the dead of night, so David got all the best bits. Reg was furious, but had he complained we could have shrugged our shoulders and said, "Well both piles were the same, weren't they, Reg?"'

It seems that the parting was as welcome to Reg as it was to Wilkie, who went on to help lay the foundations of, and enjoy the glory that was to come from, David Murray's own new team Ecurie Ecosse which was founded in 1952.

In 1950 Reg was selected by John Wyer, who ran Aston Martin's racing programme, to join the team of three cars to go to Le Mans. Reg was to become a key figure in the company's racing programme, first as a driver and later as team manager. Today a leading name in the mighty Ford empire, Aston Martin always had links with motor racing. The original sports cars built by Bamford and Martin were sold with a guarantee that each could lap Brooklands at a minimum average speed of 65 mph. The 1920s racing driver Count Zborowski drove Aston Martins back in those days and invested in the company to ensure its future, but on his death in a racing accident at Monza in 1924 the first Aston company folded. Two years later A. C. Bertelli resuscitated the company and designed a new 1.5 litre engine, giving the Bertelli cars a successful career in racing before the war.

When Bertelli left the firm in the late 1930s Gordon Sutherland took over, and during the war had the idea of producing an advanced saloon car, designed by Claude Hill and called the Atom. However, the company did not recover from the war and in 1947 the Yorkshire industrialist David Brown, who had built up his own gearbox company, saw a small advertisement in *Autocar* and for £20,000 purchased Aston Martin, saving the ailing car manufacturing company and maintaining its traditions. In the years that followed David Brown ploughed millions into the firm, and thanks to this the marque still exists today, still retaining a welcome degree of individuality within Ford.

Brown also bought the ailing Lagonda company and merged it with Aston Martin to create Aston-Martin-Lagonda Ltd. One of the reasons for this was to obtain the newly designed 2.6 litre twin-cam six-cylinder engine that had been designed for Lagonda by W. O. Bentley. It was this engine that was to take Aston Martin into motor racing.

Reg's partner with Aston Martin in the race was pre-war Le Mans veteran Charles Brackenbury, who had finished third overall the previous year with an early DB2. However, the team suffered a major setback before even reaching the course; it was Aston Martin policy to drive the actual race cars to the event, and fellow team driver Jack Fairman and his wife were involved in a bad road accident. Fairman went off the road between Rouen and Bernay and what made the accident worse was that Jack's wife was pregnant at the time and was taken to hospital very badly hurt.

John Wyer decided that Fairman, although uninjured himself, should stay with his wife at the hospital, and engaged John Gordon to take his place (he did a little racing and was later to be the Gordon part of the Gordon-Keeble GT car). This led to some restructuring of the team, and as they had brought the original factory prototype DB2 (LML 49/3) with them for just such an emergency, it was given to Eric Thomson and John Gordon to race. Reg and Brackenbury, meanwhile, were given LML 50/7, which was the car Reg was to race regularly that season, and had Lockheed rather than Girling brakes. They not only finished sixth overall but won the 3 litre class as well as the Index of Performance. Remember that this was Parnell's first race in anything other than a single-seater race car, and he found the comparable comfort of sports car racing to his liking. He thought, however, that the car was underpowered; he was later to remark that while Astons concentrated a lot of effort on Le Mans, the cars were always underpowered with their 2.6 and 3 litre engines and their good results mainly came from the handling of the cars.

Eric Thomson had been brought up in Cobham, close to Brooklands. Before the war he had been a junior member of the Brooklands Automobile Racing Club and had seen Reg race there, never imagining that he would ever go motor racing himself, or even eventually share a car with Reg.

After war service everyone received a gratuity aimed at helping them to settle back into civilian life. As Eric remembers, 'Most of us went out and spent it on riotous living, but my friend Robin Richards bought an HRG sports car, which he entered for the Alpine Rally. In September 1948 the French racing drivers club challenged the BRDC to a race at the Parisian circuit of Montlhery called "Les Douze Heures de Paris" and Robin was invited to compete with his HRG. He asked me along as number two driver; it was my first motor race.'

A year later, in 1949, Peter Clark of HRG commissioned John Wyer to build three lightweight HRGs for the first post-war Le Mans race, and Eric Thomson was one of the drivers sharing car number 35 with Jack Fairman. These needle-nosed HRGs, entered under Ecurie Lapin Blanc ('White Rabbit Team') had 1,500 cc Singer-based engines, and the Thomson/Fairman car finished eighth overall and won the 1500 cc class. It was only natural, therefore, that when John Wyer moved to Aston Martin in 1950 he should choose Eric Thomson as one of the members of the team with the original Aston Martin DB2s. Eric was able to buy the 1950 car, registration number UCM 66, and still owns it today.

The team also included George Abecassis, Lance Macklin, Charles Brackenbury and John Gordon, and Eric was clearly impressed by newcomer Reg: 'I think it was the first time Reg had ever raced a sports car in anger and he fitted into the team very well. Indeed, John Wyer told me a lovely story about the day he telephoned Reg and invited him to join Aston Martin for the 24 hour race at Le Mans.

'"What time does it start?" asked Reg.

'"Four o'clock," said Wyer.

'"And what time does it finish . . .?"'

'Reg was always considered to be the senior member of the team and the radiator grille of his car was painted red for recognition purposes. As the junior member that year my grille was painted yellow.'

During this part of his racing career Reg was always referred to as 'Uncle Reg' – particularly by Peter Collins – but his more scurrilous Derby pals such as the Ashmores called him 'The Porker', which had nothing to do with his physical shape but the fact that he raised pigs. Indeed, on a later occasion at Le Mans when Reg went off the road in the Aston Martin, John Wyer asked him why he went off.

'Oh, I was thinking about the pigs,' he said with great candour.

In all Eric Thomson co-drove with Reg Parnell four times, at Le Mans, two Goodwood Nine Hours races and the TT at Dundrod. Despite being thick-set and weighing around 14 stone, Reg was very nimble on his feet and could out-sprint most of the other drivers except perhaps Moss, who was always one of the quickest. Reg also had hands like hams, but held the steering wheel very delicately.

In May 1950 Reg received probably the greatest recognition of his driving ability when he was offered a drive in one of the factory Type 158 Alfa Romeos, at that time the outstanding grand prix car of its day, at the European Grand Prix at Silverstone.

This race went down in history as the first grand prix to take place under the new World Motor Racing Championship, which was created in 1950. Not only that, but it was also graced by the presence of His Majesty King George VI and Queen Elizabeth – the only time a reigning monarch has ever visited a grand prix in Britain. Reg, entered in the all-conquering Alfa Romeo team, was one of the drivers introduced to the King and Queen, which made it a very special occasion for him.

Looking back on it today, Tim Parnell is under the impression that the Alfa Romeo engineer Giulio Ramponi had something to do with the choice, aided of course by the British Racing Drivers Club who wanted a British driver in one of the key cars. Reg himself realised what a great honour it was, as it was the first time a British driver had been invited to drive in a foreign grand prix team since Dick Seaman and Mercedes-Benz before the war.

Perhaps realising that Reg knew the circuit and would be driving in front of his home crowd, the Alfa team tactically gave him a higher rear axle ratio so he was not in a position to truly challenge for the lead. He was also told that he was expected to come fourth, but Fangio's engine blew and he finished third. His only problem came when he hit a hare on one of the straights, but racing cars in those days were big, heavy and strong, so it did no great damage.

An excited young Tim Parnell was at the race: 'We used to stay at the Grand Hotel in Northampton and I remember that Luigi Fagioli, who drove in the Alfa Romeo team, was a very good pianist and he would sit down at the piano in the evening after practice and we would have a good sing song.'

The Alfa Romeo did 1.5 miles to the gallon and carried 110 gallons of fuel in a large tail tank, two side tanks and a saddle tank over the driver's knees – but Reg still had to stop twice for fuel and tyres! Looking at the rear of the Alfa at the start of the race the wheels were widely cambered, but when the fuel level went down they slowly became vertical and the drivers had to adapt to this situation. This was something that Reg was particularly good at, as he could adapt to cars particularly easily. Maybe it was those early experiences as a young teenager being thrown behind the wheel of strange lorries and buses.

Chapter 6

1950-1951:
BRM And Vanwall

DURING 1950 REG Parnell joined BRM as a test driver of the original V16 version. The saga of the BRM has been told so often that it does not bear repeating save to say that it was hailed to be Britain's potential world beater but eventually became the motor racing equivalent of the *Titanic*. It was beautifully engineered and very advanced for its time and might have worked with today's knowledge and technology, but placed in the context of a Britain struggling to recover from a war and a euphoric Socialist Government that wanted to transform society at the stroke of a pen, it simply had no chance. The funding came from a Trust of industrialists within the motor industry, each with his own axe to grind, and the organisation sometimes came close to proving the truth of the saying that a camel is a horse designed by a committee. But Reg Parnell was a man totally devoted to the concept of a British grand prix car, and when asked to test and race the BRM he of course agreed. He was therefore entered to race it in the Goodwood Cup on 30 September 1950, a sprint event covering 12 miles.

Reg was fastest in practice despite the wet, and led the race from start to finish, which must have brought a sigh of relief to the beleaguered BRM team, but in the second race for the Goodwood Trophy, an event twice the length, Reg had much stiffer opposition from Prince Bira and Baron de Graffenried with their Maseratis. However, again Reg got out in front and won so clearly that there was great optimism within the team that they had at last quelled the problems of misfiring and all the other troubles already associated with the car. Indeed, such was the enthusiasm of the Trust members, desperate to show that their faith in the car was justified, that they prevailed upon Raymond Mays to enter two cars for the non-championship Barcelona Grand Prix four weeks later. The drivers were to be Reg Parnell and Peter Walker.

After all, even if there were problems with a race of grand prix length, at least the team would now have had some experience of what they were up against and could work on it over the winter prior to the 1951 Grand Prix season. The reasoning and logic appeared sound – only the results did not help matters.

During practice the cars ran quite well, but in the race Peter Walker stalled his car, being unused to the high-revving engine, and although he restarted he was well out of the picture. Reg, meanwhile, had taken fourth place behind the factory Ferraris of Alberto Ascari, Piero Taruffi and Dora Serafini. This was a brilliant performance as he had started at the back of the field and had stormed past no fewer than 17 cars on the opening lap. The car sounded wonderful and clearly it was up to the task of challenging the Ferraris, but it was not to last. A supercharger drive shaft sheared and the car came to rest. Meanwhile, despite problems with the carburettor Peter Walker was doing the same as Reg and passing cars quickly on his way up the field. On the 33rd lap he was lying fifth and might have gone higher had the gearbox not split and the car pitted with oil everywhere.

Typically, the BRM project was criticised roundly by anyone with an opinion, but what was forgotten was that Britain had never really produced a grand prix car before and certainly not a grand prix car that had such technological complexity. It must also be remembered that Britain's post-war industrial recovery was slow and there were not the 'fast-track' engineering companies with expertise and knowledge that were to emerge 20 years later.

Then there was the problem of money. The BRM Trust never seemed to work and money was always short. When the Trust was disbanded in favour of a Committee led by the keenest of the investors, things appeared to be better, but world events were intruding: the Korean War had started, and this diverted many suppliers to the war effort.

It had not been Reg's best season – he only won once with his Maserati and had the two sprint wins in the BRM. His third place in the British Grand Prix, however, more than made up for this apparent lack of success.

For the 1951 racing season Reg still had his 4CLT/48 Maserati and there was always BRM in the background, but things were not looking good on that front. He opened the season with a win in the Chichester Cup at Goodwood in the Maserati, but his visit to San Remo later that month was a disaster as he retired the Maserati after only 16 laps when the rear axle failed; the starting money just about covered the cost of the trip.

When he returned to England he was approached by racing enthusiast Tony Vandervell of the Vandervell Thin Wall bearing company. He was running his own Ferrari 375 as the 'Thinwall Special' using his own thinwall bearings which were to become the established norm for engine bearings in the future. Vandervell could quite genuinely be called a 'character'. His father was C. A. Vandervell, who founded the giant CAV electrical group, he was wild as a youth, did not attend to his school work too closely, and loved motor cycles; he dabbled in racing in the 1920s with a Talbot and competed in the Senior Isle of Man TTs with Nortons.

Tony was set to work at CAV and he generally picked up a liberal engineering and electrical training in the company. Although it was not apparent at the time, he was also developing a good sense for business. However, rather than pass on the CAV group to his son, Vandervell senior sold the electrical business to Joseph Lucas, within which group CAV is still a major player.

This move did not go down well with Tony, and he left Lucas to go out on his own in the gramophone and radio business, but this was scuppered by the slump of 1929. By a tortuous route partly linked to a contact he had made in racing, he became a director of a company called O&S. When he first heard about a new development in bearings using thin shells developed in Cleveland, Ohio, he crossed the Atlantic and on the voyage met up with the chief experimental engineer for Studebaker, which was already experimenting with these new Clevite bearings. Armed with his business card as an introduction, he went straight to the Cleveland Graphite Bronze Company and eventually persuaded them that he could finance the purchase of the expensive and specialised equipment needed to produce these new bearings, provided he got the sole European rights. Thus armed, and with the backing of his father, who realised that his son had found a promising new development, the huge investment was made and Vandervell Products Ltd was created, a company that was to make Vandervell a multi-millionaire like his father.

By the time the Second World War ended – during which Vandervell had equipped military vehicles with his thinwall bearings – Tony was one of the first people approached by Raymond Mays to join the consortium to fund the development of the BRM. He did so, but the evolution of the BRM was taking so long that he decided to buy one of the Italian grand prix cars of the period, first to race and second to allow the BRM technicians to inspect their opposition at close quarters. Alfa Romeo would not sell one of their Tipo 158 grand prix cars, so Vandervell turned to Enzo Ferrari, who was using thinwall bearings in his grand prix cars.

Then there was trouble with the Board of Trade. In those early post-war years Britain was a bureaucratic nightmare, which made it difficult if not downright impossible to import foreign goods. However, the Board accepted Vandervell's argument that he had to have this grand prix Ferrari in Britain in order to research bearing production for high-speed racing engines, and they granted the permit without customs duties and tax provided that the car was only used for research, was re-exported at the end of one year and did not race! Vandervell balked at that and went back to the Board, who then said it could race provided that it was entered by the British Motor Racing Research Trust and not Vandervell Products. Incensed, Vandervell decided to pay the tax and the duty so that he was free to use the car as he wished.

The whole of the Vandervell and Vanwall saga is brilliantly told in *Vanwall* (by Denis Jenkinson and the late Cyril Posthumus, published by Patrick Stephens Limited), which is recommended reading. Suffice to say here that there were essentially three 'Thinwall Specials' – as the Ferraris were called – and Reg was asked to drive the third. This was a Ferrari 375, but with the 4.5 litre unsupercharged V12 Ferrari engine that was fitted to the chassis of the car Vandervell had used in 1950, and with de Dion rear suspension.

Reg was asked to race the car in the BRDC Daily Express International Trophy race at Silverstone on 5 May 1951. As there was a full complement of four Alfa Romeos present with Dr Giuseppe Farina, the 1950 and first World Champion, Juan Manuel Fangio, Consalvo Sanesi – Alfa Romeo's test driver – and Felice Bonetto driving, the opposition was the best available. Vandervell wanted to see how his new Ferrari would fare against them, as there were no factory Ferraris entered.

In practice Fangio broke the lap record, set the previous year by Giuseppe Farina also in an Alfa 158, but as he had borrowed Bonetto's car for this effort the surprised Bonetto found himself on the front row of the grid with Fangio relegated to the second row due to his practice time with his own car!

In the first heat and in the excitement of the moment Bonetto literally stood on the start line with wheels spinning, and Fangio shot past him from the second row into the lead. He was 5 seconds ahead of Bonetto at the end of the first lap, with Reg right behind Bonetto. Four laps later Reg swept past the Italian and began to trim Fangio's

12-second lead. Fangio responded with a quick lap, but Reg kept pushing and eventually finished just 3 seconds behind him.

Farina won the second heat and broke the circuit record, but ominous black rain clouds began to form and by the time the cars lined up for the final the heavens opened and the circuit was awash. There was hail, lightning and heavy rain, but the race was started nonetheless. Drivers had a tough time with hardly any visibility, and at places the track was covered from side to side in 6 inches of water. Bonetto's plugs were flooded and both Fangio and Farina in their Alfa Romeos were struggling, although still averaging 60 mph in conditions that would never be tolerated in a modern grand prix.

Reg, in the Thinwall Ferrari, was in his element and he not only caught up with the leaders but also passed them to take the lead, followed by the equally brave Duncan Hamilton in his Lago Talbot. All this happened in just six laps, then the Stewards decided that enough was enough and put out the chequered flag, giving Reg one of his greatest wins at an average speed of over 65 mph.

After the race Reg said, 'It's a pity it was stopped as I would have liked the race to have continued. I was a minute ahead of the Italians and I am sure they would not have made this up. It was like aquaplaning in an ice-cold tub, but in the cockpit it was very hot and steamy so that at 80 mph I only had a dim outline of the corners and only the outlines of spray telling me that another car was in front.'

Tim Parnell, who was at the event with his father, says that very few people know that Reg actually spun the car during the race – no television monitors in those days – and Reg himself kept quiet about it. However, the following week he went into the Steering Wheel Club in London to find a large blow-up photograph of him spinning, which had been caught by just one photographer, so his cover was blown!

Reg's victory made everyone sit up and take notice, and of course gave Tony Vandervell something to get excited about; he immediately entered Reg for the Festival of Britain Trophy at Goodwood a couple of weeks later. This time Farina was driving a 4CLT Maserati, as Alfa Romeo had not entered a car for the event. Reg won the first heat and created a sensation by breaking the outright circuit record on his first lap from a standing start! In the final he won again after a tremendous battle with Farina, where they took turns at breaking the lap record. It ended up in Reg's hands.

Four weeks later Reg was back in the same car at Dundrod for the Ulster Trophy. Farina was expected at this event with his Maserati, but clearly the drubbing he had suffered at Goodwood had had its effect and he arrived with an Alfa Romeo 158.

Once again Reg and Farina swopped fastest laps in practice, but the Italian, sitting back in the cockpit with arms outstretched, had the better start and took the lead with Reg running second. This was partly a tactical move, because Farina knew that he would need a fuel stop, whereas Reg could run the race without stopping. As Farina pulled away from the pits after his fuel stop Reg shot past into the lead, but just over a lap later Farina ate up Reg's 3-second lead, passed him and won the race, Reg taking second.

Although Reg had signed a contract to race the 'Thinwall Special' with Vandervell, he was also still under contract to BRM, and this took precedence. At last BRM announced they would race in the French Grand Prix at Reims with Reg, so Tony Vandervell offered his car to Brian Shawe Taylor, one of Britain's good racing drivers of the day. However, as BRM again failed to show up and as Shawe Taylor was clearly not up to the job, Vandervell offered the Thinwall to the now unemployed Reg, who in the face of a full grand prix field, finished in fourth place. To put this into perspective, no other British driver had finished as high up in any post-war classic grand prix race.

Reg drove the car again at Goodwood, taking second place, and finished his season with Vandervell by winning the Scottish Grand Prix (sic) at the bumpy airfield circuit at Winfield with the latest version of the 'Thinwall Special' with a long 'nostril' added to the bonnet to give a ram effect. (Incidentally, this was the last race meeting held at that Scottish circuit, as in 1952 activities moved about 3 miles away to another relief airfield called Charterhall.)

Meanwhile Reg's BRM contract remained in the background; it was for him perhaps more than just a driving job as he felt strongly about British participation in grand prix racing. He had been advised by BRM that the first event of the 1951 season might be the French Grand Prix, and that he would be paired with the experienced Prince Bira, but although testing showed promise, the complicated engine was still not right so the French event was bypassed, which had allowed him the drive for Vandervell. However, pressure was on for the cars to appear at the British Grand Prix in July.

It was all very last-minute, with the mechanics working right up until practice. Peter Walker was brought in to partner Reg and both drivers were told to limit the revs of the engine just in case they had the same troubles. However, another problem arose previously unnoticed due to lack of testing and racing mileage: the cockpits became like hothouses due to the exhausts passing too close to the cockpit sides, and both Reg and Peter had their legs wrapped in burns dressings to avoid their skin burning. Indeed, during the race even the rivets in the steering wheel became blisteringly hot and burned the drivers' hands. Then there was the problem of fumes in the cockpit due to an airlock when refuelling.

At the British Grand Prix the main battle was between Ferrari and Alfa Romeo, so attention was turned away from the BRMs. Again the cars seemed promising, with Parnell lapping at Farina's pace of the previous year's race, despite holding the revs down. This led to the decision by the team to go for it, and if the engines blew they blew, but at least some idea of the competitiveness of the cars would be gained against the best available opposition.

However, by this time both Walker and Parnell were suffering badly from the heat and the fumes and were having to concentrate so hard that neither saw the pit signals and both continued to the end on lower power. Reg, like Peter, ended up with badly burned legs and his hand cut from the kick-back from the steering, but his fifth place finish must rate as one of his finest and grittiest grand prix drives. While at Silverstone earlier in the year he had the perfect car in imperfect conditions, now he had a decidedly imperfect car in perfect conditions, yet he finished in the points and ahead of one of the factory Alfa Romeos driven by Consalvo Sanesi. Peter Walker finished in seventh place. What must be remembered is that neither driver was on the same rung of the ladder as Ascari or Gonzalez, yet with grit and determination they at least gave BRM a result that they could mark down as invaluable experience.

The Italian Grand Prix at Monza saw more problems for BRM, and they only just got to the circuit in time. Peter Walker was still suffering from the burns he had received from the car in the British Grand Prix, and after a struggle with the RAC and the race officials test driver Ken Richardson was given the necessary permission to drive Walker's car. For Reg the first problem was the collapse of a big-end bearing in practice; some of the correct spare parts were not available, so the mechanics had to improvise. Richardson came off at the Lesmo and bent the steering arm; as if to take pity on their rivals, Alfa Romeo helped out with repairs so that when they restarted the team was lapping Monza at a respectable average speed of over 113 mph. Then the RAC stepped in and sent a cable forbidding Richardson to drive, while back at the track the team ran out of their own fuel and had to get some local fuel, which did not react well with the engines.

The ever-resourceful Raymond Mays realised that the veteran German driver Hans Stuck – father of the present-day Hans Joachim Stuck – was at the circuit as a spectator and persuaded both him and the organisers that he should take Richardson's place. But the troubles were not over: Reg had problems with the supercharger on his car, and it was loaded on to the lorry and returned to England.

Although Stuck was driving quickly his gearbox started to overheat; again the team were discovering, race by race, the problems that should have been found through a proper testing programme in England. In hot weather and on fast circuits like Monza the lubrication system on the car was just not up to the job.

Mays then had the idea of sending someone after the lorry to pillage the gearbox from the now defunct Parnell car, but realised that it was probably a design fault and if the gearbox seized in the race on such a quick circuit the results could be disastrous. The team also abandoned a plan to test the cars at Monza after the event, and left the circuit in dejection before the race even started. In subsequent calculations, the formidable technical editor of *Motor*, Laurence Pomeroy, concluded that on its practice performance the BRM was around 6 per cent slower than the Alfas.

They say it never rains but it pours. Now the whole rules of the game changed. Having won the 1951 Championship Alfa Romeo withdrew from grand prix racing, leaving Ferrari almost unchallenged. It is said that Alfa realised that the new Ferrari would probably have the edge on them in 1952, and to pull out while at the top was the wise thing to do.

This, then, left Ferrari's opposition as the faltering and still not competitive BRM and cars like the Lago Talbots, now rather long in the tooth and unable to compete. As a result the sport's ruling body decided to suspend the existing Formula 1 for cars of 4.5 litres unsupercharged and 1.5 litres supercharged and replace it for the 1952 and 1953 seasons with what was then Formula 2, for 2 litre unsupercharged and 1 litre supercharged cars.

At a stroke the BRMs were therefore technically obsolete for grand prix racing, although there would still be a number of races for the existing cars as they were big, made all the right noises and were good for promoters of some of the lesser events around Europe. Alfa Romeo's withdrawal also meant that BRM could go fishing in deeper pools for driving talent, and they created a major coup by signing Juan Manuel Fangio and later Froilan Gonzalez – even local hero Stirling Moss. The various experiences of these drivers with BRM have been well chronicled, but the result for Reg was that he was pushed aside by the rush of big names. Yet he held no bitterness, despite having soldiered with BRM on through the bad times.

Chapter 7

1952: Aston Martin

IN SEPTEMBER 1951 Aston Martin's new sports racing car, the DB3/1, was completed. It had a tubular frame with independent trailing arm suspension at the front and a de Dion rear axle. The front suspension differed from previous Aston Martins in that transverse torsion bars were used rather than springs. The engine was a developed version of the 2.6 litre, with triple 35 DCO Weber carburettors and boasting 140 bhp. The gearbox was a five-speed David Brown unit. The bodywork was all aluminium and it was an open roadster. It had a complete undertray with air ducting to cool the inboard rear brakes, and the front grille was of the then fashionable 'egg-box' design. What was important was that the car weighed some 250 kg less than the DB2. It did not look fast and was certainly not the most successful car Aston Martin ever built, and was only raced for one season.

The car's international debut was the RAC Tourist Trophy race on the bumpy Dundrod circuit, one with which I became familiar thanks to the Royal Air Force: early in 1953 I was posted to Dundonald, ironically right beside the hairpin on the old Ards circuit, so was able to continue my journalistic work at the TTs in 1953 and 1954. As I remember it, Dundrod was always wet, and it may come as little surprise to learn that the hills around the circuit was the catchment area for all the rainwater that supplied the city of Belfast.

As the laws of the Ulster Government allowed the closure of public roads for motor racing, the Dundrod circuit was a road course along narrow Irish roads with high grass banks and deep ditches. It was therefore not a circuit for the faint-hearted, and as a result many well-known drivers feared the place. They were indeed wise to treat it with respect, for it was to prove to be a killer in all senses of the word.

Stirling Moss was brilliant there, as was the under-rated Irish driver Desmond Titterington, but Juan Fangio hated the place.

The first major race at Dundrod was the 1950 Ulster Trophy race for grand prix cars, which was won by Peter Whitehead driving his Ferrari. The Tourist Trophy race took place a few months later, but there were no foreign entrants in the event, even though it was an international meeting. This was the race when Stirling Moss came to the fore driving his Jaguar XK120 brilliantly in pouring rain to win.

The following year the entry was much better and there were a few foreign names on the entry list, but again it was Stirling Moss who won, this time in a C type Jaguar. It also saw the debut of a lone Aston Martin DB3 in the hands of Lance Macklin. He had the car in second place before the exhaust system came loose and he had to come into the pits to have it fixed. Sadly the car retired with seized bearings as a result of the car's Elektron alloy sump having expanded and contracted so much that it loosened the securing bolts, producing a leak in the gasket. The English driver Eric Winterbottom was killed when he crashed his Frazer Nash, and veteran driver Eddie Hall was severely injured when his Ferrari went off the road: so Dundrod's deadly reputation began.

Four years later, in the 1955 TT, when there was the most spectacular entry for any post-war sports car race in Britain, no fewer than three drivers were killed and the race never returned to the circuit. Today Dundrod is still used for motor cycle racing, and on a recent visit I had to shake my head in astonishment that cars were ever raced there with literally no safety facilities and a potential danger every 100 yards.

Reg Parnell had no grand prix drives in prospect for the 1952 season, and the change of formula left everyone looking for cars to race. He did have a couple of races with a Cooper-Bristol and there was promise of the odd British national race in a BRM, so the main emphasis was on his contract with Aston Martin. A new man joined the team that year, motor cycle racing champion Geoff Duke. In 1951 he had been presented with the Sportsman of the Year trophy, at which event Lord Brabazon had asked him if he was interested in racing cars. Geoff was actually quite keen, and Brabazon arranged a test with John Wyer in an Aston Martin. Wyer had actually seen Geoff on a motor cycle at the British industry proving ground at MIRA and had been impressed, so he invited Duke to come to MIRA for a test with a lightweight DB2. Although Duke had asked that John Wyer did not time him, Wyer actually did and found that he was only a second slower than the best time they had recorded with the regular team members in a DB2.

After his drive Geoff, one of the most calm and quietly spoken individuals, told Wyer that it was different but felt that given time he could get the hang of it. He then went out again and was quicker than any of the team drivers at MIRA, so Wyer immediately signed him up. He also signed for that season a young up-and-coming driver called Peter Collins whom he had seen in action at the TT driving an ungainly and unhealthy looking Cadillac-Allard.

That year a sports car race was held on the Monaco Grand Prix circuit, but it was a disaster for Reg and for many other drivers, so much so that it was the last sports car race to be held on the street circuit.

The DB3s were using the new 3 litre engine and there were a lot of teething troubles. Indeed, John Wyer summed up the race in his report: 'Our troubles in this race, which we might easily have won, were due to insufficient time being allowed for test and development.'

During the event Reg's engine blew as he approached Ste Devote, but he managed to get the car stopped alongside the straw bales without doing too much damage. However, he had spread oil over the circuit and the leader, Frenchman Robert Manzon in a Gordini, lost control on the oil and smashed into the Aston Martin to be followed seconds later by Stirling Moss in his C type Jaguar. Moss only just jumped out of the car in time before Hume's Allard went straight into the growing pile of scrap. When the wreckage was removed it was found that Reg's Aston Martin DB3 was now a full 3 feet shorter!

The real problem was that Aston Martin, as usual, had driven the race cars to Monaco, and were due at Le Mans ten days later to race in the 24-hour event. Clearly Reg's car was in a mess and there was no time to get it back to Britain to be repaired, so it was sent by train to Paris and the workshops of the famous coachbuilders Henri Chapron. As a precaution another DB3 with a coupé body was sent out to Le Mans to take its place, and was used in practice.

All the Aston Martins had reverted to the old and more reliable 2.6 litre engines for Le Mans, but the problems were not over. Pat Griffith, brought into the team for the race, crashed his DB3 heavily during second practice. Wyer immediately telephoned Chapron to say that they needed the car desperately at Le Mans; Chapron had almost finished repairs, but these had left it with a decidedly shortened tail. Marcel Blondeau, owner of Aston Martin's concessionaires in Paris, actually drove the car by road to Le Mans so that it could start in the race.

Those familiar with Le Mans regulations will realise that the car could not legally race as it had not been scrutineered and had not practised for the event, but come 4.00 pm on the Saturday the stump-tailed Aston Martin DB3 lined up on the starting grid. Nobody said anything, even though Wyer was sure that Lofty England, the manager of the Jaguar team, realised what was going on. However, the Le Mans organisers didn't, so the car ran in the race, although it was to retire.

Due to his motorcycle commitments Geoff Duke only drove four times for Aston Martin in 1952, although he was re-signed for 1953. Roy Salvadori, who later took Geoff's place in the Aston Martin team, has very strong views about Geoff: 'Geoff Duke never had a chance . . . he was a fabulous driver and was pushed in at the deep end and really needed a year playing around in the minor races getting experience. I think at the time most of the Aston Martin team were against him, the main reason being that he got an awful lot of publicity. Peter Collins, for instance, never courted publicity but somehow the publicity Geoff was getting got right up his nose and I think that is what started the bad feeling.

'With motor cyclists in those days they were coming into motor racing as stars and so were expected to do well immediately, and to his credit at Berne, during his first season in 1952, he was absolutely sensational and made everybody sick!

'I replaced Geoff in the team and he just missed out on the DB3S, which was a shame as it was a much better car.'

John Wyer, in his book *Racing with the David Brown Aston Martins*, alludes to this when he says, 'I know that my opinion of Duke's abilities as a driver differs from that of most contemporary observers and the generally accepted judgement is that he was a very great motorcyclist who failed to make the transition to cars.

'I maintain that I had more opportunity to evaluate him than anybody else and I am convinced that he had great potential.

'Temperamentally, he had difficulty in settling down in the team and certainly the established drivers did nothing to make it easier for him. Not unnaturally they resented the fact that he got more publicity than they did . . . but I will always regard Geoff Duke's early retirement as a loss to motor racing.'

In his very first race, at Goodwood, Geoff finished second in the DB3, then came Berne. What must be remembered is that he knew every bump and twist of the Berne circuit, as he raced motor cycles there. He and Reg were given lightweight DB2 Aston Martins, and pitted against them were four of the new Mercedes-Benz 300SLs and two factory Lancia D24s.

During practice Geoff was not happy with the handling of his car and asked to borrow Reg's. He immediately set fifth fastest time, the four cars in front being the factory Mercedes. However, due to the rules it was Reg who started the race from fifth position, as it was his car that had qualified highest; Geoff was further back in the field.

Geoff tells a nice story about this incident. Geoff asked Joe Craig, who prepared his successful Nortons, to watch the practice from a particular bend and give an opinion of his driving. Afterwards Craig said, 'Your driving was very good. But in the second session Parnell was really flying through there!' Of course, it had been Geoff in Reg's car.

Although he started on the back of the grid, Geoff's car was much better and he picked off some cars on the first lap. Then Caracciola's Mercedes, lying in fourth place, hit a tree, which fell on to the road so the field had to queue up to get past; meanwhile the leading three Mercs got so far in front that they almost lapped the tail-enders. Geoff ended up fourth overall.

Geoff decided to take up car racing for 1953 and was put into a DB3 alongside Peter Collins at Sebring. On the flight out Reg was keen to see the Empire State Building, but as the Lockheed Constellation flew over New York there was a lot of low cloud and he never did see it.

In the race Collins took the lead then handed over to Geoff, who hit a slower car and spun off into an oil drum and the car was retired. This did not help the atmosphere in the team, as Peter Collins had some strong remarks to make to John Wyer about the competence of his team mate. Geoff came back from Sebring very depressed, and when Graham Walker (father of commentator Murray and editor of *Motor Cycling* magazine) rang to say that he had the chance to ride a Norton, he jumped at it. He had another race at Silverstone in the Aston Martin DB3 when the clutch failed, so he took a decision he had avoided in the past, being loyal to Norton, and signed for the Italian Gilera team. David Brown let him out of his Aston Martin contract and that was it.

Geoff Duke was to return to car racing some years later and raced the factory Gemini during 1960 in Formula Junior. Even today, when talking to him about car racing, you get the impression that perhaps Salvadori was right and he really had all the cards stacked against him.

At the 1952 Le Mans Reg and Eric Thomson shared an odd DB3 Coupé. This was the original DB3/1 on to which Aston Martin's Frank Feeley had designed a fastback roof. This was welded on to the body and the car rushed off to Le Mans where it missed Wednesday practice while the gearbox was changed.

Eric Thomson describes the famous running start at Le Mans: 'I watched from the pit counter as the drivers lined up on the other side of the road waiting to sprint across to their cars when the flag fell. Reg was a burly figure, but very nimble, and he was across the road and into the coupé ahead of the other Astons. He was leading them at the end of the first lap but at the end of the second Peter Collins was on his tail. John Wyer had ordained a lap speed of 5 minutes 23 seconds as the strategic plan for the race. The coupé had a very distinctive exhaust note and when I sat behind the pits I could hear it pass, easily complying with the plan. However, after 50 minutes there was silence. On the tenth lap the hypoid gears had failed and DB3/1 retired.'

That was really the end of DB3/1's racing life, as it was returned to the factory where the roof was taken off and thereafter it was used as a practice car for various events including the 1953 Mille Miglia.

Reg then drove DB3/3 in the Production Car race at Silverstone in a team that included Geoff Duke, George Abecassis and Lance Macklin. Geoff spun and damaged the steering, but Reg, Abecassis and Macklin finished second, third and fourth respectively to Stirling Moss's winning C type Jaguar, giving them the team prize. For the British Grand Prix Reg was offered a drive with Archie Bryde's Cooper-Bristol, which was the prototype car. Remember that in 1952 there was an interim Formula 1 for 2 litre cars so that the 2 litre Bristol-engined Cooper became eligible for the event. Parnell once again displayed his ability by finishing seventh.

During the Nine Hour race at Goodwood Thomson recalls driving the short-tailed Aston Martin DB3: 'Reg was lying third behind two Jaguars and ahead of Collins and Abecassis in the sister Aston Martins when he handed over to me. I maintained this position but became aware of a thin trail of smoke following behind. When I came in for my routine pit stop I expected to see Reg, as usual, standing on the pit counter ready to jump into the car, but he was standing on the road, and when I stopped and got out he took me by the arm and we strolled away down the pit lane. Almost immediately there was a whoosh and the Aston went up in flames. John Wyer had his head inside the boot and Jack Sopp, the chief mechanic, was under the car and both were seriously burned. The woodwork on the pits was set on fire.

Immediately Reg took charge. He moved the timekeepers into another pit and hung out pit signs to the other Astons to keep going while the shambles was sorted out. He was quite unflappable and everyone instinctively followed his instruction. We made amends the following year when we won the Goodwood Nine Hours with an Aston Martin DB3S.'

The fire also caused problems for the race leader at the time, Roy Salvadori, who was driving Bobby Baird's Ferrari. Salvadori had almost driven the race single-handed as Baird had realised that the Londoner was a much quicker driver. Roy saw the fire in the Aston pit, which was right next to the Ferrari pit, and when he next came in for tyres the team found that the fire had softened the tarmac and the jacks started to sink into the ground; as a result they could not get the new wheels on to the car. Bobby Baird's mechanics managed to put blocks under the car but they lost a lot of time.

Salvadori takes up the story: 'I went out again and was taking chunks off the leaders' times, but dear old Reg, my old mate, had us called in just after we had taken over the lead. He had seen the Ferrari had a flickering tail light and having looked at the regulations had seen that the scrutineers would have to insist the light was fixed and as a result we finished in third place . . . he made a bloody good team manager!'

By the end of 1952 the BRM Trust had had enough and put the whole team up for sale, but as a final curtain call entered Gonzalez, Ken Wharton and Reg for the Daily Graphic Trophy and Woodcote Trophy at Goodwood. Almost as though sensing that it was their last chance, the cars finished first, second and third.

Two weeks later Reg went back up to Scotland to race in the Daily Record Formule Libre race. He had many friends in Scotland: David Murray of Ecurie Ecosse, of course – even though they had slightly fallen out when Murray had taken Wilkie Wilkinson away from him – and Jock McBain, the man behind Ecosse's greatest rivals, Border Reivers. Reg had also befriended another ebullient Scottish club racer, John Brown, who had an HWM sports car, and on one occasion Reg actually raced this car in Scotland.

Ken Wharton and Reg had two BRMs, but it was an embarrassing race for them both as Bob Gerard in his ancient ERA – sold to him many years before by Reg himself – won the race from Ken Wharton, who had spun trying to catch Gerard. Reg retired with transmission trouble.

The BRM sale took place just two days later and it was almost a foregone conclusion that Alfred Owen of the Owen group would buy the team. At the Easter Monday Goodwood meeting of 1953 Reg raced for BRM alongside Ken Wharton, but had problems with the engine and finished fourth. He never drove the BRM again. Ironically his son Tim was to become BRM's Team Manager in 1966.

Chapter 8

1953-1954:
Campaigning the DB3S

REG WAS ONCE asked what he thought of the Aston Martin DB3S compared to the DB3, and his reply was, 'Well, the DB3 was, of course, a considerable improvement over the DB2, but the difference between the DB3 and the DB3S was like chalk and cheese. The newest Aston is smaller, lighter and handles even better than previous models. I believe the Avon tyres contribute largely to the superb handling. [Aston Martin were introduced to Avon tyres by Geoff Duke, who had used them on his Nortons and swore by them, and they were to remain loyal to Avon for many years.] Its compactness makes me feel much more secure when I drive, and I think its response is just about perfect. From the cockpit of the DB3S a normal road seems like an Autostrada. If there was as sports car formula – and I'd like to see a 3 litre limit – I believe the Aston Martin would be the top-ranking sports car in the world. Four and 5 litre cars are too big and powerful for modern sports car competition.'

His remarks about the 3 litre formula were to prove correct and were adopted a few seasons later, but his remarks about large-engined cars were perhaps less prophetic when one thinks of the sports cars that were to follow decades later. One wonders, for instance, what he would have made of the fastest of all sports racers, the Porsche 917 twin-turbo, which produced 1100 bhp!

Roy Salvadori had now joined the team, and as he had never raced the DB3 his opinion of the DB3S was slightly different: 'It was a notorious understeerer. The way to drive a DB3S called for extremes, and some of the time it was absolutely ridiculous. When I was given my own car I would put the tyre pressures up to 60 lbs to stop the understeer. If you see any photos you will see I kept the back out because for me it was the only quick way to drive a DB3S. Road circuits did not fit into my style with the DB3S – with the exception of Oulton Park – and they tended to neutralise me. The people who came into their own were Peter Collins and Tony Brooks – they just seemed to have the feel for road circuits. Unfortunately Reg and I suffered when we drove together at Dundrod – we were just not in the hunt with Brooks and Collins – but on the British airfield circuits we were.

'When I joined the team I was first paired with George Abecassis for a race, then Dennis Poore. Finally I was usually paired with Reg Parnell.

'I was very pleased to drive with Reg as he was the number one driver and it meant you were going to get the better machinery. Unfortunately Reg loves tampering with things and he was so used to botching things to get cars to the starting line that there was always something of a reliability factor when he got involved. Reg would always try the special cars such as the supercharged car at Le Mans, and more often than not we landed with a lemon, but he was a great guy to have in the team as he could be firm and wouldn't stand any nonsense.'

Aston Martin decided to enter the new DB3S for the Mille Miglia in 1953, but it was not their first attempt. A year before they had run two lightweight DB2s for Reg and George Abecassis, partly because in 1951 journalist Tommy Wisdom had done well there with a privately entered Aston. In 1952 Wisdom ran again as a private entrant with a DB2 against the two factory cars, and before the race Reg did a one-lap recce with John Wyer, George Abecassis and Pat Griffith using a Lagonda road car. Wisdom won the class from Reg in strange circumstances. After the last road control Reg had slowed down, thinking he had an unassailable lead, but Wisdom had been driving hard and managed to beat him by 2 minutes. Needless to say, Reg kicked himself over this . . .

When Aston Martin decided to return to the Mille Miglia in 1953 it was felt that Reg should take along a driving partner in the shape of photographer Louis Klementaski. Amongst other things Klem was the official photographer for Aston Martin and was photographing all the things a manufacturer likes to record for posterity.

Born in Manchuria, China, Klem had been a racing driver at Brooklands before the war with a supercharged J2 Montlhery MG, and later a supercharged single-seater Austin Seven. He also owned a Delage, which he bought when he helped found the Junior Racing Drivers Club (not to be confused with the Junior Car Club). This was a very early concept of a racing drivers' school, founded around 1934 and the idea of former Invicta driver Roland Morgan. Morgan had a flourishing car business selling performance cars, and his idea was that in order to help the garage pay its way he would contact some of the rich young men of the time who had sports cars and persuade them to have their cars tuned by him. As an encouragement he would offer them a racing course, and towards this end he used to hire the Mountain Circuit at Brooklands and show them how to become racing drivers. Klementaski helped with this, and once blooded on the track the young men wanted to start racing. So it brought more business to Morgan's sports car shop.

'These test days on the Mountain Circuit were really quite good as we persuaded many of the racing drivers of the day to help out as observers and tell the young bloods where they were going wrong. I remember we used to have people like Kay Petre, Anthony Penn-Hughes and Tim Rose Richards. They used to come along to the track on a Thursday evening in summer and stand around and make notes. We then used to gather them together with the young pupils and they would pass comment on the various driving faults they had seen out on the track . . . Jack Fairman was one of our early pupils.'

Today Klementaski lives quietly in an old school house in a tiny village near Bath and is working on his autobiography, which should be revealing as he ranks as one of perhaps a dozen of the finest exponents of motor racing photography in the world. Although much of his fame derived from his motor racing images, he was also a professional photographer who specialised in industrial work and theatrical photography.

The Aston Martin bid in the Mille Miglia in 1953 was a serious effort and the aim was an outright win. As a result one of the old tank-like DB3s was pressed into service as the 'mule'. The recce took a full two weeks and Parnell and Klementaski chose to split the route into two parts. One week was spent covering the northern sections and the second week the southern loop; for the northern part they stayed at L'Aquila and for the southern loop just outside Florence.

Although Denis Jenkinson has always been credited with the 'toilet roll' concept of writing the details of the route and corners on a long scroll of paper, which would then be read out to the driver, Louis Klementaski used the technique on the Mille Miglia two years before Jenkinson and Moss's famous 1955 win. (I believe that the first driver ever to use the technique was the American John Fitch.)

In an effort to give the old car a bit more performance, the DB3 'mule' was fitted with a supercharger (a DB3S ran with a supercharger at Le Mans in 1954) and the service crew used a Lagonda estate car.

'From the first week,' remembers Klem, 'I took notes on the severity of the corners with mileages to help Reg, as he could never begin to remember the whole route. I then brought these notes back and transferred them to a roll, and Aston Martin made me a box to put them in. The whole experience was a real eye-opener and I must admit to having slight misgivings. So I came to an understanding with Reg. The important thing was to finish and to take no risks. However, there were places such as over a hump-back or on certain corners were Reg might have lifted off and I was able to give him the flat-out hand sign.

'As a photographer I took two cameras with me on the Mille Miglia, but unlike with Peter Collins in a Ferrari a few years later, I only shot black and white with the Aston. At that time I only used Leicas, one with a 28 mm wide-angle lens and the other with a standard 50 mm F2 Sumar lens, which for those days was a very fast lens and gave good quality even at maximum aperture.

'Once we had finished practice I was quite happy to be driven by Reg, and with my notes we were fairly confident.'

Three DB3Ss were entered, with Peter Collins/Pat Griffiths and George Abecassis/Mike Keen in the other two. For Reg and Klem it proved to be a successful adventure, which made all the practice work worthwhile. They finished in fifth place overall, which was a tremendous performance for a British crew on normal Italian roads over a thousand miles – and with a bent Panhard rod that had pulled out during the pounding the car received during the event. Early on Reg went off the road and hit a straw bale when an official jumped out in front of him; they carried on but Reg felt there was something wrong with the steering and stopped the car. Klem jumped out and found the offside wing pressing on the tyre, so he grabbed it and pulled it hard, only to realise that it was almost red hot. Also the headlamp was damaged.

No one passed them during this brief stop, but Luigi Villoresi caught them up at the next village and went past in his Ferrari, horn blowing. They climbed the famous Futa Pass north of Florence, then on the Raticosa Reg suddenly slowed and stopped. The throttle cable had broken and it would take them 10 minutes to rig up a new cable properly, so Reg told Klementaski to open the throttle wide and tie it up that way. Klem thought he was joking, but he meant it – they completed the final few hundred miles controlling the car with the ignition switch, Reg changing gear with one hand and manipulating the switch with the other. They had a problem at the Bologna control when restarting with the throttle wide open, but luckily the starter was strong enough to get them moving and the engine fired.

As Klem recalls, 'I think it was somewhere north of Florence when the throttle cable snapped. From then on he was either flat out or switched off. By that time I was so much into the race and desperate to get on and finish that I had no qualms about this at all. This was typical of Reg because even during the practice rounds all sorts of things would go wrong and he would jump out and fix or jury-rig things; he knew everything about a car and was very practical.'

Reg and Klem were to do another Mille Miglia together in 1954, again with a DB3S, but this time they went off the road and had an enormous accident. The spot was near L'Aquila in the Abruzzi mountains. Ironically, they had stayed in a hotel near L'Aquila during the recce, so were very familiar with this stretch of road.

Klementaski: 'Although the road wound through the mountains it was not really a pass and in the race I had given Reg the grade for this upcoming right-hand corner. There was a row of white railings on the outside protecting a drop and he arrived at the corner at the right speed, but a few hours earlier one of the little Fiat 500s, which had set off early, had gone on to the verge on the inside and spewed a lot of earth and sand on to the road. Well, it acted like ball-bearings and we shot across the road at high speed. I got my elbow tucked in as I knew we were going to hit on my side. The impact tore the front wheel off the car and it was left in a sorry state. I remember photographing Reg standing disconsolately beside the wreckage.'

Klementaski did only one more Mille Miglia as a co-pilot, and that was in 1955 with the Belgian driver Paul Frère in an Aston Martin DB2/4 Coupé before joining up with his friend Peter Collins in Ferraris for 1956 and 1957.

At the 1953 Le Mans Reg was partnered by Peter Collins in Aston Martin DB3S chassis number 2, but the chances of victory were virtually nil as that year there was one of the strongest entries ever. There were three factory Alfa Romeos for a start, with Fangio, Karl Kling and test driver Consalvo Sanesi, four Lancias driven by Piero Taruffi, Robert Manzon, Felice Bonetto and Froilan Gonzalez, and four Ferraris driven by Alberto Ascari, Nino Farina, Giannino Marzotto and Luigi Chinetti, so the Italians were out in force. Then there were the factory Jaguar C types of Stirling Moss, Peter Whitehead, Duncan Hamilton and Roger Laurent, and finally the Cunninghams of Briggs Cunningham, Phil Walters and Charles Moran.

At the end of the first hour the order was Jaguar, Ferrari, Jaguar, Ferrari, Alfa, Alfa, Alfa, Cunningham, then the two French Gordinis. Also within that hour the Parnell/Collins car was out when Reg went off the road and crashed. It was on this occasion when John Wyer asked him what had gone wrong and he came out with the classic remark that he had been thinking about his pigs. But even John Wyer was to admit that the Aston Martins were not properly prepared for that event, and all three cars were to retire. Reg, however, was in absolute despair and, clearly out to make amends, asked Wyer if he could take the spare car – the original prototype DB3S chassis 01 – straight back to England, then over to the Isle of Man for the British Empire Trophy race the following weekend. Wyer put it to David Brown, who agreed, and first thing on Monday morning Reg left La Chartre with mechanic Rex Woodgate beside him and drove the DB3S to the Channel and up to his home in Derby, where he and Rex had a sleep then set off for Liverpool and the ferry to the Isle of Man. it proved to be a turning point in the DB3S's progress, Reg beating the factory Jaguars in a truly gritty drive. Indeed, that victory not only restored Reg's good spirits, but also marked a change in Aston Martin's fortunes, as the DB3S proved unbeatable for the rest of the season.

For the 1953 Goodwood Nine Hours Reg was again paired with his friend Eric Thomson. This particular race was notable for the effect that track resurfacing made on the tyres. The surface was particularly abrasive and all the teams had problems. For Aston Martin with their Avons it meant that the tyres had to be changed every hour and a half! Recalling the race, Eric Thomson felt that 'perhaps Reg was a bit under the weather because he found it difficult to maintain the pace, whereas I thrived on that circuit. Indeed, John Wyer recorded that on some laps I was taking time off Stirling Moss. Reg, however, was a realist and had no false pride, and he had the grace to suggest that for the last stint I should continue in the car and we won the event. That was very typical of him – he wasn't trying to hog the limelight.'

To many enthusiasts of the time Reg Parnell was a modern-day hero. One little boy was taken by his father to see that Goodwood race and remembers it well. When Reg and Eric arrived back in the paddock he ran forward to ask for their autographs, but neither had a pen, so they lifted him on to the bonnet of the Aston and drove round to the back of the pits where they found one and signed his autograph book. They also gave him some of the flowers from the winners' laurel wreath. Many years later that little boy became one of Britain's most successful and popular club racing drivers – Barry Williams. 'Reg Parnell was my true hero and the funny thing is I dried out the petals of those flowers, put them in a little envelope and kept them for 40 years. Then about three years ago, in a fit of cleaning up the family house, my mother found the envelope with these old dried up flowers and threw them away: a right disaster!'

Reg was clearly enjoying his racing and when asked about his future at that time he said, 'Everybody asks me about my future in motor racing. I'm now 42, and for the record I have no intention of retiring. There are days when I feel so near 21 that I think I can go on for ever, and there are days when I feel so near 60 that I think I've had it. But motor racing pays too well for me now, and although I'm building up a large pig farm in Derbyshire, I hope to stay in racing for a long time. I'll stick with Aston Martin, I think, as long as David Brown and John Wyer will put up with me . . . there is no happier way to travel from country to country than with a motor racing team . . . some other sports may be more profitable than motor racing, and most are less risky, but the feeling of clean competition in first class cars on high-speed circuits is enough to keep me in the game for a long, long time.'

If there had been problems with the resurfacing of Goodwood there were greater problems over in Ireland when the county surveyor for that little patch of roads up behind Belfast, Mr Grigor, decided that a new non-skid surface should be applied to Dundrod. This was my first visit to the circuit and I remember all the paddock chatter about tyre wear. Lofty England of Jaguar was particularly unhappy about these sharp chippings, as he felt that a set of tyres on a C type Jaguar would only last 75 miles and the race was over 111 laps, or 823 miles (sports car races in the 1950s ran over considerable distances and on Dundrod it was a true marathon for survival).

This prediction resulted in Norman Freeman, Dunlop's racing manager, organising an all-night flight of aircraft to carry tyres to Dundrod. It also sent Lofty England and John Wyer into a huddle, and there was talk that they would withdraw their cars from the event. They didn't, and the usual Irish rain began to fall, which made things a lot easier on the tyre wear. However, it was then discovered that visibility was down to 50 yards on some parts of the course, and the start was delayed for an hour and a half so that it was late evening before the long race came to an end.

The event was run on a handicap principle, and although Peter Collins in his Aston Martin led off the line, he had to remember that the tiny DB Panhards had been given 21 laps credit over the Astons and 22 laps over the Jaguars. What a hell of a way to run a motor race! If you were following the race as a handicap event it was being led by the Panhards, two MGs and Irishman Redmond Gallagher in a little Gordini. On the road Stirling Moss was leading in his Jaguar. Reg Parnell and Eric Thomson were still up there in the running. It took seven hours of hard driving for Peter Collins and Pat Griffith to take the lead on handicap with the Parnell/Thomson car in second place and the Moss/Peter Walker Jaguar third. Moss then had trouble and pulled up short of the finish line, eventually rolling across the line to take fourth place with the Aston Martins first and second.

For the 1954 motor racing season Reg Parnell bought the Ferrari 500 Formula 2 car (chassis number 188) from Isobel, the widow of Irish racing driver Bobby Baird. This was not a new car as Baird had bought it around July 1952 and had raced it mainly in British events since then. He occasionally gave it to Roy Salvadori to race and also shared his Ferrari sports car with Salvadori. Indeed, it was Salvadori who made the arrangements between Isobel and Reg for the sale of the car.

Baird had been the wealthy owner of the *Belfast Telegraph* newspaper. Indeed, when serving my National Service in the Royal Air Force my signals centre was right beside the main Belfast/ Newtownards road. As Bobby Baird lived out near Newtownards I remember not only hearing but also seeing Baird flash past the camp gates in his Ferrari sports racing car. Sadly, however, this likeable man was killed in a racing accident at Snetterton in 1953 with the Ferrari, which rolled and pinned him underneath. He did not appear to be badly hurt but simply winded; brushing off help, he started to walk back to the pits. However, he collapsed when a broken rib punctured his lung and he died later in hospital. After buying the car Reg sent it back to Modena to have a 2.5 litre Formula 1 engine fitted for the new 1954 Grand Prix formula. Around the same time there were two other privately entered Ferrari 500s, 184 owned by Rudi Fischer and 186 by Louis Rosier, and they too were uprated by the factory.

The Ferrari proved to be one of the most successful single-seater racing cars Reg ever owned. He totally dominated the 1954 British racing season with the car – and it also had other uses. Ted Cutting, Aston Martin's designer, remembers going up to Reg's workshop in Derby where he had the entire Ferrari Formula 1 engine in bits. He photographed everything and afterwards studied the design of the engine, coming to the conclusion that 'for the DBR1 we wouldn't do it that way.'

Meanwhile Reg remained a mainstay of the Aston Martin team, and in 1954 they went to Le Mans again with a polyglot selection of cars. For a start there was a DB3S for Reg and Roy Salvadori, which was different from all the rest in being supercharged. This created a great stir in the British press, but Roy was in no doubt about the car.

'Probably it was Reg who talked John Wyer into the idea of supercharging the car, but it was only mildly supercharged as otherwise the engine would not have lasted. It really did not have much more power and in fact it was nothing startling at all and was very low-key. Eventually the engine gave up after 21 hours. It was typical of Reg, always wanting to try the special cars . . .'

The other cars were two experimental DB3S Coupés for Peter Collins/Prince Bira and Graham Whitehead/Jimmy Stewart. The race proved these to be aerodynamic disasters, both of them having spectacular crashes near White House and almost within sight of each other.

Jimmy Stewart, who cut his teeth racing for Ecurie Ecosse in the C type Jaguar his father bought for him, was very quick and was voted as one of Britain's most promising racing drivers by *Motor Racing* magazine. He used to come to some of the race meetings with his little brother Jackie, who many years later was to emulate Jimmy's performances and become one of the world's greatest racing drivers.

Jimmy Stewart had taken up John Wyer's invitation to drive for Aston Martin at Le Mans partly out of pique, as he had hoped to be chosen by Jaguar due to his exploits with their cars with Ecurie Ecosse. Being such a nice guy, with more than a touch of innocence, when he arrived at Le Mans he asked Peter Collins's advice about driving the circuit and in particular the fast kink on the Mulsanne Straight.

'Until I actually got to Le Mans for practice I had never even driven an Aston Martin road car, far less a racer, and my first impression was that it was so much slower than my normal C type Jaguar. In fact, I was given a black mark by team manager Wyer when he asked me what I thought of the car and I said, "Well, to be honest I wish I was driving my C type as I would be a lot quicker", which was perhaps not the most diplomatic thing to say in the circumstances. In my ignorance I asked Peter Collins about the kink on the Mulsanne and he told me it was absolutely flat out. I tried a few times and it appeared impossible, but eventually I became very brave and took the kink flat out. When I came back to the pits Peter said to me, "You didn't really take it flat did you? I was only joking"'

The other car entered was the large Lagonda DP (Design Project) 115, which was an attempt by Aston Martin to go into the big league with a large-engined car. It used a 4.5 litre V12 engine and was given to Eric Thomson and Dennis Poore to drive. The engine was developed by William Watson alongside Professor Robert Eberan von Eberhorst, who had been given permission to come to Britain after the war and worked with ERA before joining Aston Martin. As a former engineer involved with the Auto Union grand prix cars before the war, he carried impressive credentials, although the resultant V12 engine had basic design faults. It was fitted to a similar chassis to the DB3S but with a much longer wheelbase and slightly wider track.

Reg was the first person to race the Lagonda DP115 in the sports car race supporting the Silverstone International Trophy in 1954. Although he finished in fifth place, the car did not seem to have any greater potential than the existing Aston Martin DB3Ss. When it went to Le Mans with Eric Thomson it proved to be very quick in a straight line but poor in cornering, and was actually slower than the DB3S.

'It was built specifically as a Ferrari-beater' remembers Eric. 'It was a pig and its main problem was that it just wouldn't go round corners – it went straight on. It was remarkably fast down the straight but on the corners the understeer was terrible. Going into Tertre Rouge you could see my front wheels were almost at right angles to the car turning into the corner . . . I spun the car and crashed it. I keep getting reminded of this accident when they show the film *Dance With A Stranger* on television [the story of 1950s racing driver David Blakely who was murdered by his girlfriend Ruth Ellis, the last woman to be hanged in Britain] and they used the film footage of my crash in the Lagonda as part of the Le Mans sequence. I think more people know about that than anything else.'

Despite this setback a second Lagonda chassis was completed and again it was given to Reg to drive in the sports car race supporting the British Grand Prix at Silverstone. This time he finished fourth, which would normally be regarded as progress except that the regular team Aston Martin DB3Ss finished first, second and third!

This was the last time a DP115 was raced, and the cars might well have been chopped up but for the intervention of the British film industry. A motor racing movie called *Checkpoint* was being planned starring square-jawed British actor Anthony Steel. Aston Martin sold both cars to the producers of the film and they appeared in disguised form. In the late 1980s both of them came back into private ownership. The body of one of the later Lagondas found its way on to a Tojeiro chassis, and in the 1990s Scottish enthusiast Tom McWhirter re-created one of these Lagondas and hoped to race it some time in the future.

For the 1954 Tourist Trophy the Ulster Automobile Club had a re-think about the handicapping system, feeling that the little cars were still given too tough a task, so their handicap became even more favourable. Added to that, they reduced the length of the race. Luck was with them because one of the World Sports Car Championship events at Nurburgring had been cancelled, which threw the spotlight on the Ulster race and brought in all the factory might. Lancia, who were now racing against Ferrari for the championship, fielded a strong team with drivers like Alberto Ascari, Juan Manuel Fangio and Piero Taruffi. Jaguar were also out in strength with the D types, and Ferrari had Gonzales, Trintignant and Hawthorn in their cars.

Aston Martin were also there, but clearly they were going to have a struggle this year, and Reg and Peter Collins drove their hearts out to take fifth and seventh places. However, bucked by the handicap system, Rene Bonnet and Elie Bayol in their tiny little DB had an 11-minute lead over the fighting racers behind them, led by Mike Hawthorn's Ferrari with Piero Taruffi and Fangio in their Lancia in second place. But it was the racers that the crowd was looking at, not the ungainly little DB that was actually leading the race. Even when poor Bonnet and Bayol crashed in the wet conditions and team mates Gerard Loreau and Paul Armagnac took over the lead in the other 750 cc DB, nobody seemed to notice. They came home the winners but the real laurels went to Hawthorn and Fangio who had their own remarkable race for the lead. Both Collins and Reg retired from the race, but everyone was beyond caring. The farce of the little 750 cc car that could only record 100.0 mph along the flying kilometre when Ascari's Lancia was timed at 144.6 mph underlined what a ludicrous result this was for a World Championship event. As far as I am aware a handicap system has never again been used in a world event.

Chapter 9

1955-1957: Connaughts, and Retirement

DURING 1954 DAVID Brown took the decision to enter three of the new Aston Martin DB2/4s in the Monte Carlo Rally. John Wyer had been contacted by the famous and successful Dutch driver Maurice Gatsonides, and as Gatso was in great demand Wyer signed him up for the team. The other drivers were Reg Parnell and Peter Collins. (A few years earlier Peter Collins had competed in the Monte with Ecurie Ecosse founders David Murray and Ian Stewart with a Ford Pilot, but that had been very much just a bit of fun.) Gatso's co-driver was Frenchman Marcel Becquart, and Collins took along fellow racing driver Graham Whitehead. Reg was to be accompanied by Louis Klementaski.

When he won the Monte in a Ford Zephyr some years before, Gatso had used Tyresoles, an English retread tyre development with wires embedded in the tyres to give more grip in icy conditions. He suggested this to Aston Martin, but due to their now strong association with Avon they had to turn down the idea; however, Wyer was able to persuade Avon to produce a special 16-inch snow tyre with a similar tread pattern to that of the Tyresole – a pattern which, incidentally, had not been patented.

In November 1954 Gatsonides tested these tyres on one of the original DB2s from Le Mans in 1951 (XMC 76), but time was tight and when he set off to find some snow he found that the knobbly Avons were 'chunking'. However, Avon was able to change the compound before the event and the teams prepared to set off.

By no stretch of the imagination could Peter Collins or Reg be called specialist rally drivers, and on snow and ice they did not exactly shine, with Peter finishing 95th and Reg 153rd, which is why it is hard to find their names in the results – or indeed in many contemporary reports. Gatsonides, on the other hand, finished fifth overall, despite being penalised 180 points in a secret road check to see if the competitors were maintaining the correct average speed (Gatsonides was running 18 minutes early).

Louis Klementaski has his own happy memories of that event: 'We had chosen to start from Munich and had a few days out there before the start. As there was an opera house in Munich and as I was very keen on opera I saw there was a performance of *Madame Butterfly* taking place on the first evening. So I said to Reg that I really couldn't miss this opportunity of seeing opera as there was not so much around at that time, so did he mind if I went to the opera? He surprised me by saying, "I'll come with you." It was such an incongruous idea, but he asked me to get two tickets and arrived with this girl. So the three of us went to the opera and of course he just couldn't understand it. Mind you the performance at the Munich Opera that night was pretty bad . . . it was a most dreadful performance.'

As for the rally: 'It was quite an eventful run. We left the start with Reg saying he would drive . . . and promptly drove for 19 hours non-stop in terribly icy conditions. Then he said, "I've had enough, you take over", and promptly went to sleep. I drove for about five hours and at the next control he said he felt all right and took over the driving again.

'We had been given keep-awake pills – Benzedrine I suppose – and as I cannot bear to be driven fast round corners in a closed car I thought I had better take one of these. Being terribly tired at the time and in such a daze I forgot to start the stopwatch on the last test before the Nice control. However, on this stage Reg got the bit between his teeth and caught up with a Porsche and he was driving like the wind. As a result of this we arrived at the control three-quarters of an hour early! When we got there John Wyer greeted us and I was in such a daze I just wandered off and when we were due to check in nobody could find me as I was just wandering about all over the place.'

Early in the year John Wyer had held a couple of test sessions at Chalgrove to try out new drivers, and amongst these were John Riseley-Pritchard, Don Beauman – who had also been tested by Jaguar – and a young dental student called Tony Brooks. As a result, Brooks, who had been racing a Healey Silverstone and a Frazer Nash Le Mans Replica up to that time, was signed.

For the 1955 Le Mans race Aston Martin were still running the DB3S and were rewarded with a superb second place by Peter Collins and Paul Frère. Two other DB3Ss were entered for Tony Brooks/John Riseley-Pritchard and Roy Salvadori/Peter Walker, but they both retired. Reg, on the other hand, was entered with Dennis Poore in the Lagonda DP166, which looked more like an enlarged DB3S than the bloated and ungainly Lagonda DP115 of the previous year.

After the relatively poor showing of the earlier Lagonda it is surprising that Aston Martin took the experiment further, but during the winter Watson, assisted by Ted Cutting, redesigned the chassis. This became the DP166, and two were built specifically for Le Mans. As it turned out one of the entries was withdrawn, but the other was driven by Reg.

That fateful 1955 Le Mans was dominated by the tragic disaster when over 100 people were killed in Pierre Levegh's accident. Luckily for Aston Martin, this diverted attention from their poor performance and it was the last time the Lagonda name was used on a racing car. However, for those who like happy sequels, the two DP166s were used as 'mules' for the development of the DBR1 Aston Martins and, as we know, these were much more successful. At least Reg had been the only driver who had given them any results; if you look at his racing history, remarkably he seemed able to bring results from fundamentally unsuccessful cars.

To modern-day motor racing enthusiasts the name Connaught Engineering probably means very little, but this small company, based at Send in Surrey, has a permanent niche in the European motor racing Hall of Fame. It was the Connaught that took a young English driver, Tony Brooks, to victory in the Syracuse Grand Prix of 1955 and provided Britain with its first International grand prix win since Seagrave's Sunbeam more than 30 years before. It was also a monumental victory in another sense, in that it gave new impetus to a British motor racing scene that was still recovering from the embarrassing disaster that had been the BRM; everyone appeared to take heart and makes like Cooper, Lotus and Vanwall were all to emerge within the next six years as not only grand prix winners but also World Manufacturers' Champions, so establishing the centre of grand prix car manufacture and technology firmly in England. The fruits of the work of pioneers like Connaught can be seen today, with the whole world coming to Britain for its motoring technology and development.

The power behind Connaught was Rodney Clarke, who ran Continental Automobiles Ltd; he was a perfectionist whose racing cars were always well made and strong, if perhaps a little too heavy. Talk to any racing driver who raced a Connaught and he will tell you that it handled beautifully but never really had enough power. With today's technology applied to the Connaughts racing in current historic events we are now seeing the car's great potential being realised; it was a pity that it did not have the horsepower it deserved, as it might well have won many more races at a grand prix level.

Luckily, in the early development years of Connaught, Clarke was asked to prepare a pre-war Maserati for Kenneth McAlpine, of the construction company. McAlpine was interested in Clarke's plans and became his benefactor, providing the money to build the cars. Despite this Connaught was always scraping the barrel in the manner in which most British racing car companies conducted business back in these post-war days of severe financial restrictions.

The engine used by Connaught came from Geoffrey Taylor's Alta company, which had built racing cars before the war and which had raced not only on the home front at Brooklands but had also made occasional forays abroad for the voiturette races that usually ran alongside grand prix events much in the way that Formula 2 was to evolve in the 1950s. The post-war Alta engine was developed towards the end of the war as a supercharged 1.5 litre to fit in with the proposed new rules for grand prix racing whereby engines had to be 4.5 litres unsupercharged or 1.5 litres supercharged. This formula not only got grand prix racing off the ground after the war but also created the monumental battles between Alfa Romeo and the newly born 4.5 litre Ferraris and the legendary, fragile and ultimately futile 16-cylinder BRM. For the 2 litre unsupercharged Formula 2 class, however, Alta used a revised version of the engine with four SU carburettors.

For the 1954 racing season Connaught had hoped to have a new V8 Coventry Climax engine, but it did not come into production. Searching round for an alternative, Rodney Clarke decided to use Alta engines, but developed by Mike Oliver who worked with him at Connaught and occasionally raced the cars himself. Their 2.5 litre Alta engine, which equipped the B type Connaughts, was probably the most developed version and they were running with twin-choke Webers, having dabbled with fuel injection but in the end deciding in favour of the more familiar carburettors. When the car appeared it was fitted with a streamlined body, which made it look even bigger and heavier.

In September 1955 Reg was approached by Connaught and offered a drive in one of the two factory streamlined cars at Aintree alongside Jack Fairman. The streamliner was built along the lines of the Mercedes-Benz grand prix cars of the previous season, but Mercedes had scrapped the streamlined body as even Fangio found it difficult to aim into the corners, and an open-wheeled version was preferred.

The Aintree race was a non-championship event for the Daily Telegraph Trophy and Reg was at the top of his form, leading the race from the fall of the flag. Then two laps from the end the car ran a bearing and Roy Salvadori's Maserati rushed through into the lead. As usual the gritty Reg did not give up, and eventually coasted round before jumping out and pushing the car over the line to be credited with sixth place, a lap down.

Rodney Clarke, like Mercedes, decided that Fairman's car (B1), which had been damaged against a concrete post at Aintree, should be rebuilt as a normal open-wheeler and given to Reg to drive at the Gold Cup race at Oulton Park. Again Reg put in one of his gutsy drives, but was no match for Stirling Moss in a factory Maserati who won the event. Mike Hawthorn took second in a Lancia – one of the cars inherited by Ferrari when Lancia withdrew from grand prix racing – Irishman Desmond Titterington finished third in one of the new Vanwalls developed by Tony Vandervell, and Reg was fourth.

When the chance came for Connaught to go to the Syracuse Grand Prix, a chance enhanced by some pretty good starting money, the team prepared two of their B types to go to the event, but Reg was not one of the drivers. Instead Clarke chose a young sports car driver called Tony Brooks, together with Les Leston, who had already raced Connaught sports cars with success. This was to be a triumphant event that was to raise British hopes for future grand prix success. Brooks, despite opposition from the factory Maseratis, won the race and set the foundation for what was to be four decades of British ascendancy in grand prix racing and the construction of racing cars. Bearing in mind the large part that Reg had played in the whole reconstruction of motor racing in Britain after the war, and his willingness to go out and race hard to achieve victory, it was a great pity that he had not been the driver, but that is to take nothing away from Tony Brooks's brilliant win.

Tommy Sopwith, racing driver and son of famed aeroplane manufacturer and America's Cup yachtsman Sir Tom Sopwith, offered Reg his Connaught-engined Cooper Bobtail. This was a streamlined sports car based on the single-seater Cooper, which was later to evolve into the Cooper Monaco. The race was at Snetterton at the end of the season, but Reg had problems with the clutch and could only finish second. He also drove a Cooper-Jaguar at the same meeting.

For the 1956 Tasman Series Reg appeared with a single-seater Aston Martin that had been in the melting pot a long time. The priority for David Brown and Aston Martin had always been to be successful with sports cars, but as early as the 1951/52 close season they had considered the design of a Formula 1 car using a 2 litre engine (the interim Formula 2 design used in the World Championship for two seasons), but no real effort was made and the chassis was scrapped. However, the new 2.5 litre Formula 1 of 1954 caused Brown to re-consider the design, and towards that end a narrowed DB3S sports car chassis was used for the experiment with one of the 2.9 litre engines reduced in capacity to 2.5 litres. However, as we now know, the new formula brought Mercedes-Benz back into racing, and it became clear from the start that this Aston Martin effort would not be competitive, so the plan was abandoned.

However, at the end of 1955 Reg had the idea of rebuilding this car with a supercharged 3 litre DB3S engine, but this blew up in testing and a 2.5 litre unsupercharged engine was put in its place. By using alcohol fuel they managed to get horsepower figures similar to those of the supercharged engine. The car was shipped out to New Zealand, but at the first event at Ardmore the engine blew again in practice. As this was a Formule Libre event, Peter Whitehead offered Reg his Cooper-Jaguar sports car to race, and he finished in fifth place.

Two weeks later in the Lady Wigram Trophy race Reg took the Aston Martin to fourth place behind the Ferraris of Peter Whitehead and Tony Gaze and the streamliner Connaught of Leslie Marr. During the series Reg became very friendly with Tony Gaze, the Australian driver who had raced for a number of seasons in Britain with a variety of cars including the ex-Whitney Straight Maserati, an Aston Martin DB3 and a DB3S. However, there was another slight link that brought them together. During the war Gaze had been flying in Britain and had met Kay Wakefield, wife of pre-war racing driver Johnny Wakefield, who was a test pilot for Vickers. Tragically Wakefield was killed in a flying accident when testing a new plane; as we know Reg bought his 4CL Maserati from Kay, and Tony had seen Reg race the car in Jersey in the late 1940s. Tony later married Kay Wakefield.

During this Tasman Series Tony and Reg travelled together, and Tony was able to introduce him to some new forms of sport.

'Reg had never been a fisherman. I took him out fishing and he soon got the hang of it and every so often that familiar Derbyshire voice would ring out "Got woon!"'

Tony was also with him on the occasion that Reg was invited to visit a local government pig farm and meat works in New Zealand. After showing them round, the Director took them for a drink and casually asked Reg what he thought of the pigs. Taking a swig from his glass, Reg looked him in the eye and said, 'Couldn't sell them boogers in England.'

As Reg had raced a Ferrari 500 during the 1954 season he was very familiar with them, and as Tony Gaze was having trouble with his, Reg helped him clear up a flat spot problem in the engine.

At one of the events Reg was entered for the sports car race in an Aston Martin DB3S, while Tony was in his HWM-Jaguar, and this was the only occasion when Reg played a trick on him. 'There was a Le Mans start for this race and I thought he was trying to help me when he told me he had put my HWM-Jaguar into gear. He had . . . trouble was he had put it in reverse so everyone shot off and left me. Luckily the HWM was quicker than him so I won the race anyway.'

As Reg and Kay Gaze got on very well, she asked him why Tony had never been offered a factory drive with Aston Martin in any of the long-distance races, as he had consistently been quicker than Graham Whitehead's DB3S. She was told that it was felt that Tony didn't take racing seriously enough!

When he had bought his Aston Martins Tony Gaze had dealt with John Wyer – this was before Parnell joined the company. 'John told me when I had my DB3 that no new model was on the way, but at the final meeting of the year out came Reg with the DB3S, then when I had my DB3S the next thing I knew Reg came along with a new multi-plug head, but later Reg told me he had an agreement with Aston Martin that he would be given the fastest of the factory cars.'

The Aston Martin single-seater venture was not a great success and in the Australian Grand Prix on 2 December Reg could only finish sixth behind Moss and Behra in Maseratis, Whitehead in his Ferrari and the Maserati 250s of Hunt and Stan Jones.

However, the concept of building a Formula 1 car was not forgotten and during 1956 work began on the car that was to become the DBR4. Again this project was to take a back seat for a couple of years while Aston Martin concentrated on sports car racing with the developing DBR1.

The 1956 racing season was to prove to be Reg's last. During the 1955 season Rob Walker, probably one of the most successful private entrants in grand prix racing during the post-war period, with many grand prix wins to his credit – something a modern-day private GP team can only dream about – had decided to buy a B type Connaught (chassis number B4), and had success with it driven by Tony Rolt. He asked Reg to drive the car for the Glover Trophy race at Goodwood on 2 April 1956, but he finished a lowly fifth. Reg won the handicap event, but finished third overall due to the handicapping system.

Three weeks later he was entered in the same car for the BARC 300 at Aintree, but retired. At the same meeting he ran in the production

The much-modified, re-bodied and supercharged MG Magnette raced by Reg Parnell for two seasons until he lost his racing licence at the end of the 1937 racing season. (Tim Parnell Collection)

Reg Parnell's racing album

When Reg was brought before the RAC Tribunal that led to the loss of his competition licence in 1937, he was represented by Oliver Bertram QC, who was himself a well-known racing driver at Brooklands and became the second fastest man ever to lap Brooklands driving the Barnato Hassan Bentley. (Graham Gauld Collection)

LEFT *Reg gets a push start in his BHW at Brooklands during the 1939 season.* (Tim Parnell Collection)

BELOW *Brooklands, 1939: Reg and Kay Petre have a chat after his licence was returned to him following a year's ban due to his accident with her.* (Tim Parnell Collection)

RIGHT *Reg gives his old friend Leslie Brooke a few hints about the Brooke Special.* (Tim Parnell Collection)

BELOW RIGHT *Reg trying hard at Donington in 1939 with his newly acquired BHW* (Tim Parnell Collection)

Reg's own grand prix car, the Challenger, photographed in 1947 when it was fitted with the Delage engine. It was a very professional-looking racing car and was similar in appearance to the contemporary 4CL Maserati. (Ludvigsen Library)

The Delage engine fitted in the Challenger. (Ludvigsen Library)

The Grand Prix des Nations at Geneva in 1946, with Reg's ex-Wakefield 4CL Maserati about to lap Eric Verkade's odd-looking Talbot 700. (Tim Parnell Collection)

LEFT *Freezing in Sweden, February 1947: Reg gets a push start before going out to win the race at Rommehed, the first of two ice races. For the second race Reg had a set of twin rear wheels sent over from England.* (Tim Parnell Collection)

ABOVE *To fend off the Swedish cold most of the drivers used ex-RAF flying jackets. Photographed before the ice race are Reg, Prince Bertil of Sweden, Leslie Brooke and George Abecassis.* (Tim Parnell Collection)

BELOW *Reg is given the chance to drive one of the pre-war Mercedes-Benz grand prix cars at an unknown location. Along with Joe Ashmore and Rob Walker he almost managed to buy one of the 1.5 litre supercharged Mercedes.* (Tim Parnell Collection)

In July 1946 Reg went to Albi for the
Grand Prix there. At a local restaurant he
has a meal with his business colleague Fred
Ashmore (left) and Motor sports editor
Rodney Walkerley (right). (Tim Parnell
Collection)

Albi Grand Prix, 1946: Fred Ashmore
raises his hat to the camera while Reg tries
on a new one. On Reg's left is his cousin
Roy Parnell. Reg raced his Maserati in this
event while his Delage, seen here, was
raced by David Hampshire. (Tim Parnell
Collection)

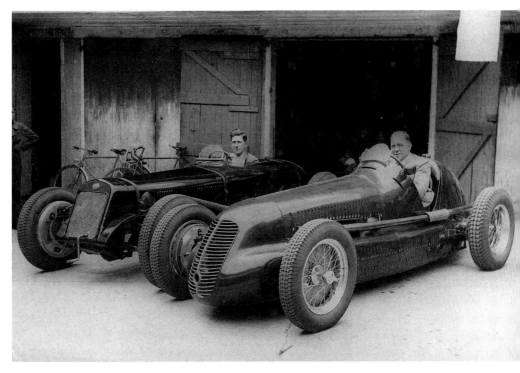

The Parnell équipe at Albi in 1946. David Hampshire is at the wheel of the Delage, with Reg in the 4CL Maserati. (Tim Parnell Collection)

An atmospheric shot during practice at Albi: No 20 is Reg's Maserati, while the other Maserati 4CL partly hidden by the mechanic is Tazio Nuvolari's car entered by Enrico Plate. On the right is Harry Schell's Ecurie Franco-Americaine 6CM Maserati. (Tim Parnell Collection)

LEFT *The famous moment during the 1947 Ulster Trophy race when Reg lost control of his Maserati 4CL to let Prince Bira in his ERA win the event. Bira glances over his shoulder and can't believe his eyes.* (Dineen, Tim Parnell Collection)

BELOW LEFT *The starting grid for the 1947 Jersey Road Race. On the front row are the four Maserati 4CLs of Raymond Sommer (far side), Louis Chiron, Nello Pagani and Bira. On the second row are Bob Ansell (Maserati), Bob Gerard and Raymond Mays in their ERAs. Reg's Maserati on the third row is obscured by the pit crew, but on the right can be seen the E type ERA of Peter Whitehead.* (Tim Parnell Collection)

RIGHT *Joe and Fred Ashmore with their ERA at the Jersey Road Race.* (Tim Parnell Collection)

BELOW *First time in South America: Reg at the wheel of his 4CLT Maserati in Argentina, 1949.* (Tim Parnell Collection)

Victory at Zandvoort for Reg in his Maserati, 1949. For once he is almost dwarfed by the huge laurel wreath. (Tim Parnell Collection)

Reg at speed in the wet with the original BRM. He was the first person to win a race with a BRM and was also one of the test team. (Graham Gauld Collection)

Fred Ashmore and Reg Parnell helped to raise money for charities, such as at this dinner attended by many racing friends. Left to right the gentlemen are Peter Collins, Stirling Moss, John Heath (HWM), Fred Ashmore, Reg Parnell, Leslie Brooke, Ken Wharton, Bertie Bradnack and journalist Barclay Inglis. (Tim Parnell Collection)

The tight corner at Onchan village on the Isle of Man, with Reg at ease in his 4CL Maserati. (Tim Parnell Collection)

ABOVE *For a big man Reg Parnell was unusually quick off the mark at Le Mans starts. Here he is almost in the cockpit ahead of Tony Rolt in the Jaguar C type at Silverstone, July 1953.* (Tim Parnell Collection)

BELOW LEFT *Aston Martin's team headquarters for Le Mans were at La Chartre, and before the race there was time to relax. This picture, taken prior to the 1955 event shows, left to right, Peter Collins, Roy Salvadori, John Riseley-Pritchard, Peter Walker, Reg Parnell and Tony Brooks.* (Roy Salvadori Collection)

BELOW RIGHT *Somewhere in Italy on recce for the 1953 Mille Miglia, Reg adjusts the tyre pressures on the Aston Martin DB3 while Pat Griffith holds the umbrella. The Competition Department's Lagonda chase car is also in attendance.* (Tim Parnell Collection)

The Aston Martin team live it up in a pub at Le Mans in 1957. Among those in the picture are mechanics Eric Hind and Jack Sopp, Reg Parnell, The Honourable Gerald Lascelles (left, clapping), former team driver Eric Thompson (in dark suit, also clapping) and behind him Aston Martin PR man Alan Dakers. (Gillian Stillwell Collection)

High jinks at Le Mans, 1957. This is the infamous wine-drinking race with Reg just pipping his cousin Roy to the post. On the left Pat Griffith eggs them on. (Gillian Stillwell Collection)

TOP LEFT *It ain't 'alf wet, Mum: some idea of the conditions at Silverstone in 1951 when Parnell drove Tony Vandervell's Thin Wall Special Ferrari. The race was eventually stopped, with Reg declared the winner.* (Tim Parnell Collection)

MIDDLE LEFT *Master of the wet: Reg in the first of the Aston Martin DB3Ss just at the point of aquaplaning.* (Tim Parnell Collection)

BOTTOM LEFT *With the exhaust trailing Reg drives the Aston Martin DB3S on the Isle of Man during the British Empire Trophy Race, 1953. Note the proximity of the spectators to the racing.* (Graham Gauld Collection)

ABOVE *A rare photograph of Reg testing the original Aston Martin single-seater, but fitted with the supercharged DB3S engine.* (Gillian Stillwell Collection)

BELOW *Reg had problems with the car during testing, and had to be rescued by Roy Parnell with a DB3S. Reg has his finger in his mouth as if to say, 'Oh, what have I done?'* (Gillian Stillwell Collection)

Just before the start at Christchurch, New Zealand, during the 1955 Tasman Series, Reg is about to climb into the bulky looking Aston Martin grand prix car. In the background Peter Whitehead in his Ferrari moves up to the front row of the grid. (Tim Parnell Collection)

Dunedin, New Zealand, during the 1955 Tasman Series, with Reg in the Aston Martin single-seater (No 1) second in line. In the foreground is his friend Tony Gaze with his Ferrari 500 grand prix car. (Tony Gaze Collection)

Real airfield racing during the 1955 Tasman Series, with Peter Whitehead and Tony Gaze leading in their Ferrari 500s followed by Leslie Marr in the streamlined Connaught and Reg (Aston Martin) taking the outside line. (Tony Gaze Collection)

Reg in the Lagonda DP166 specially built for the 1955 Le Mans 24-Hour race, looking very much like a 'blown-up' DB3S. (Alain Mathat Collection)

Le Mans, 1956: the Aston Martin team lined up in front of the pits with the Moss/Collins car, which finished second, in the foreground and the Walker/Salvadori car behind it. Part hidden is Aston Martin No 14, the prototype DBR1 raced by Parnell and Brooks. (Tim Parnell Collection)

The Aston Martin pits at Le Mans during practice. David Brown and John Wyer confer while Stirling Moss listens in. On the right, wearing glasses and standing behind the Salvadori/Walker Aston Martin, is Roy Parnell. (Tim Parnell Collection)

Team tactics at Le Mans, 1957. Reg is by now team manager; on the left are factory drivers Tony Brooks and Roy Salvadori, and on the right privateer Aston Martin drivers Henry Taylor and Graham and Peter Whitehead. (Roy Salvadori Collection)

There are times when a man just needs a drink. Reg caught having a swig of wine before the start of the 1,000 kms race at Nurburgring in 1957. (Gillian Stillwell Collection)

Reg searches out a problem at the Nassau Road Races of 1957 with Stirling Moss and the Aston Martin DBR1. (Gillian Stillwell Collection)

Stirling Moss had a way with Aston Martins on the Nurburgring, and here in 1958 he tells team owner David Brown and Reg about his victory. (Gillian Stillwell Collection)

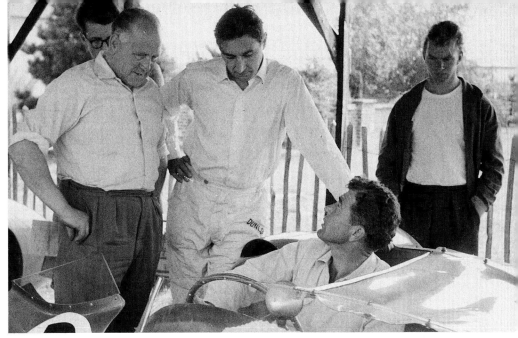

Goodwood, 1959: Reg and Roy Salvadori compare notes with Carroll Shelby. (Roy Salvadori Collection)

A photograph taken at the Aston Martin factory after the 1959 Le Mans race and marked 'Not to be used'. The caption reads: 'This shows a heavy pitting mark on a pinion tooth. In actual fact approximately 4 teeth were in this condition, equally spaced at approximate intervals of 4 teeth, ie every 4th tooth was in this condition. Aston Martins state that the cause of this was mis-alignment.' (Tim Parnell Collection)

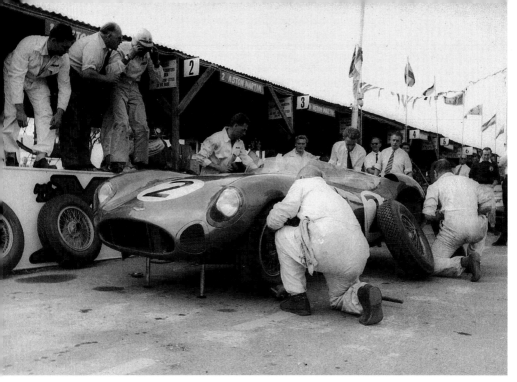

ABOVE *Pit stop at Goodwood, 1959: Reg, on the pit counter, gives final instructions to Carroll Shelby who is adjusting his goggles. In the background Jack Sears (in the dark sweater) looks on. Note the air jacks in operation.* (Graham Gauld Collection)

BELOW LEFT *Tourist Trophy Race, 1959: Reg in his familiar sunglasses has words with Roy Salvadori. Standing with the camera is American photographer Jesse Alexander, and behind him is the Duke of Richmond and Gordon, owner of Goodwood.* (Graham Gauld)

BELOW RIGHT *The Aston Martin DBR4 on the rolling road before it went racing.* (British Petroleum, Tim Parnell Collection)

Aston Martin raced the DBR4 grand prix car during 1960. Roy Salvadori is congratulated by Reg and (foreground) David Brown, owner of Aston Martin. (Roy Salvadori Collection)

John Surtees tests the first Yeoman Credit Cooper at Goodwood early in 1961. Reg is seen at the rear right with his back to the car. (Gillian Stillwell Collection)

Riverside, 1961: Reg feeds a porpoise watched by (left to right) Innes Ireland, Roy Salvadori, John Surtees, John Cooper (part hidden, taking a picture), and American racing driver Ruth Levy. (Gillian Stillwell Collection)

German Grand Prix, 1962: John Surtees confers with Reg about practice times at the Nurburgring. (Gillian Stillwell Collection)

Prior to the 1962 US Grand Prix at Watkins Glen, 19 of the racing cars taking part were loaded aboard BOAC's initial flight CL44 to New York. Among the cars are the factory Lotuses, BRMs, Bowmaker Lolas, Coopers and a BRP Lotus. (Gillian Stillwell Collection)

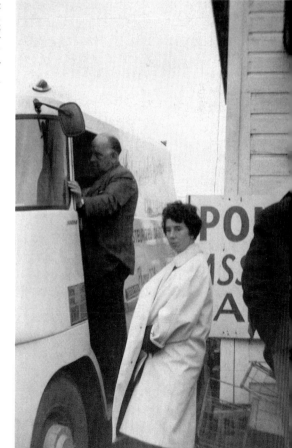

After the 1962 Grand Prix at Watkins Glen, Reg and his secretary Gillian Harris had to go to this milk float to claim their starting money! (Gillian Stillwell Collection)

This otherwise unremarkable photograph of Reg presenting trophies at a local car club dinner is interesting in that the tall youth on the right holding the tiny cup for winning his class in a driving test meeting is David Hobbs, who went on to be successful in all forms of racing and is now a motor racing commentator in the USA. (Tim Parnell Collection)

Tim Parnell at a Mallory Park club meeting in August 1957 with his Bobtail Cooper sports car. This was one of his first races. (Tim Parnell Collection)

Tim's Lotus 18 Formula Junior at Mallory Park in 1961. (Tim Parnell Collection)

Reg smiles the smile of a proud father as son Tim is presented with the Bryant Trophy at Snetterton after winning with his F2 Cooper. (Tim Parnell Collection)

Graham Hill and Jackie Stewart confer with Tim before one of the races in the 1966 Tasman Series. (Tim Parnell Collection)

Tasman Series, 1966: Jackie Stewart in the BRM retires from the event at Levin. Tim Parnell was guest team manager for the Series. (Tim Parnell Collection)

Tasman Series 1966: Jackie Stewart seems to be drowning his sorrows as Dickie Attwood gains the laurels for winning with BRM. Tim Parnell and his wife Virginia are in the background. (Tim Parnell Collection)

Motor racing has changed in the past 30 years. Team manager Tim Parnell strips off and gets down to work on Jackie Stewart's BRM during the Tasman Series. (Tim Parnell Collection)

Jim Clark (centre) seems to be saying, 'Now, nobody move – I've just dropped a sixpence and I want you all to look for it.' Among those searching are Jackie Stewart (left), Frank Gardner (with foot extended), Dickie Attwood and Tim Parnell. (Tim Parnell Collection)

A meeting of Les Anciennes Pilotes *in 1986 brought together Tim Parnell (right), Paul Frère (centre), and pre-war German ace Manfred von Brauchitsch. (Tim Parnell Collection)*

saloon car race with Rob Walker's Mercedes-Benz 300SL against a new young Swiss driver called Jo Bonnier in an Alfa Romeo 'Disco Volante', which could hardly be termed a production saloon.

Just prior to the saloon car race Stirling Moss rushed up to one of the bookmakers at the circuit and put £5 on Reg to win; the bookmaker accepted the bet with a raised eyebrow and refused any more bets! Reg won by a country mile and Stirling collected.

At the International Trophy at Silverstone in May with the Connaught he retired again, this time with gearbox trouble, so perhaps he was beginning to feel that the writing was on the wall. After all, he had been racing for more than 20 years, and there was the farm to look after. He was no longer competing in grand prix racing and most of the drivers who had raced alongside him, like his friend Luigi Villoresi, had retired.

Le Mans came round again in July and following the disaster of the previous years the pits had been rebuilt and there were many changes aimed at safety. However, the FIA decided that Le Mans would no longer count towards the World Sports Car Championship, but then, as today, it was just too famous to be ignored by the major manufacturers. For Aston Martin it was also a time to run their newest toy, the DBR1, which made its debut there and was given to Reg to drive along with newcomer Tony Brooks. For Stirling Moss, returning to the team that year after his races with Mercedes-Benz, Le Mans was an important event and John Wyer paired him with Peter Collins in a 3 litre DB3S; they were to finish in second place to the Ecurie Ecosse D type Jaguar of Flockhart and Sanderson only 10 miles behind the winners after 24 hours of racing.

The Le Mans regulations put a limit of 2.5 litres on 'Prototypes', so the DBR1 could not run with its 3 litre engine, and had to make do with the smaller unit. Despite this it had a promising debut and ran as high as fourth place overall, but in the final hour, in seventh place the back axle broke. It was the last car to retire from the race and it must have been a withering disappointment to the team; however, at the same time it demonstrated the potential of the new car for the future.

It was another disappointment for Reg, but a race meeting at Crystal Palace was coming along and he concentrated on preparing for that. Reg would always confide in his old friend and entrant Rob Walker, and prior to this race he told Rob that he was determined to beat Stirling.

'That B type Connaught was a shocker to get off the line,' Rob Walker recalls today. 'I actually spun it at the start of the Brighton Speed Trials and that takes a lot of doing. Reg, however, was a lot better than me, but at the start at Crystal Palace he got the car sideways then tore off determined to catch and pass Stirling in the 250 F1 Maserati.'

Reg was clearly annoyed at such a silly mistake and drove flat out on the opening lap, but in trying to outbrake Moss the car locked up and went off the road into Crystal Palace's unyielding railway sleeper barriers.

'When the ambulance brought him in from the circuit his face was white and he looked terrible,' said Walker afterwards.

Reg had broken his collarbone and did not do much racing after that. However, Rob Walker's faith in him had not disappeared, for when he was in hospital recovering Rob came to visit him and asked his opinion of the new Cooper that had just been announced.

'Get one immediately,' said Reg, and during the conversation he told Rob that he had heard that Stirling Moss had had a disagreement with his chief mechanic Alf Francis. Rob then contacted Francis and offered him a job in his team.

'Alf was not really interested and wanted to get out of motor racing as he had had enough and didn't want to go motor racing any more. However, I offered him a cottage in the country and the opportunity to be his own boss with complete control over the team, so he joined us at Rob Walker Racing.'

Reg and Rob also discussed drivers for the new Cooper, and Reg recommended Tony Brooks, who had been badly injured racing a BRM in the British Grand Prix that year.

Walker duly bought the Cooper Type 41 Formula 2 car and gave the recovered Brooks a drive at Oulton Park in September that year where Brooks finished a brilliant second to Roy Salvadori's factory car and ahead of Ron Flockhart in the John Coombs-entered Lotus.

The following season Brooks was signed by Tony Vandervell to drive the Vanwall. He later joined Ferrari and had a brilliant career that almost saw the shy and retiring driver become World Champion. Like many of the characters encountered in this book, Brooks is almost forgotten today, yet he was one of the greatest racing drivers Britain ever produced.

At the end of the 1956 season Reg was in touch with the Ferrari factory and a deal was agreed whereby he would return his 2.5 litre 500 and in return would get one of the unsuccessful Ferrari 555 Super Squalos, which were about to be replaced by the Lancia-Ferraris. Parnell wanted to compete in the 1957 Tasman Series, so the Super Squalo was to be fitted with one of the big four-cylinder 860 sports car engines. Peter Whitehead agreed to take the only other

Super Squalo left at the factory with the same configuration, also for the Tasman.

The cars were taken to New Zealand where they were very successful. They were then sold to private owners there, who continued to race them, while Reg returned to England, unsure about the future. After all, he had the farm and the garage business and a growing son, so he had plenty to keep him busy.

The accident at Crystal Palace had a strong effect on him, and when the opportunity came to move to the other side of the fence with Aston Martin he took it. John Wyer was moved upstairs within the Aston-Martin-Lagonda group to become General Manager, and as a result of this Reg was asked to join the company to replace him as team manager for the 1957 season.

At the same time his friend and racing colleague Eric Thomson also retired from racing; he became one of Reg's part-time team and continued to go to Le Mans as a member of the timekeeping group and part-time 'gofer'.

Chapter 10

1957-1958:
Team Manager and
Magical Moss

AS REG WAS going to take on this greater responsibility at Aston Martin he needed some help behind the scenes, and that was to arrive in the comely shape of Gillian Harris, who was to assist Reg in his motor racing exploits for the rest of his life.

Speak to anyone who was in the Aston team at the time and they will tell you that Gillian was the real power behind the throne, who handled all the administrative work that Reg found tedious. At the same time Reg had John Wyer with him at races as moral support, but Wyer made sure he did not interfere with Reg's plans and would even wait until the last moment before arriving at a meeting. As Eric Thomson recalls, 'I once said to David Brown that I had never heard him give any orders at a race meeting. He smiled and said, "You should hear me at board meetings." I suspect John Wyer applied the same principles with Reg.

'Reg had no enemies in the team and worked quite happily with the mechanics before the races, but even before then, when John Wyer was in charge, he would invariably discus tactics with Reg, appreciating his blunt appraisal of the situation.'

Gillian Harris grew up near Staines and after finishing school completed a bilingual secretarial course at the Institut Français du Royaume Uni in South Kensington, her fluency giving her an edge in the job market.

Initially she was interested in joining one of the airlines, preferably BOAC (now British Airways), but when she discovered that it was their policy to start all secretarial staff in the typing pool she quickly changed her mind. Her first full-time position was with the Standard Motor Company (later Standard-Triumph) in the export department at their Berkeley Square showrooms. She became expert in handling the complicated customs documents that had to be completed if a customer wished to export a car from Britain. In addition at weekends she worked with one of the salesmen who had set up his own business on the side, selling performance equipment mainly for Ford and Austin cars for club racing. Initially she thought she would leave Standard to join him full-time. However, his plans did not work out, and he told her of an advertisement he had seen in *Autosport* for a Competitions Secretary at Aston Martin. The regulations that existed in those days for the export of cars almost exactly matched those for the temporary export of cars, engines, transporters, equipment, etc., and her experience obviously gave her an advantage. She therefore went for an interview with John Wyer and Reg at the Aston Martin offices in Piccadilly.

'I had accepted the job before I actually visited the Hanworth Air Park at Hounslow where Aston Martin had their service, experimental and racing workshops and offices. It had been used by the RAF during the war and many of the buildings were rather decrepit and ramshackle, to say the least; the toilet facilities were in a completely separate building. I was told later that someone had been offered the job before I applied – she took one look at the place and decided not to accept!

'I was interviewed by both John Wyer and Reg, although I never actually worked with John Wyer. I am not sure I could have survived that. He was a very difficult man, extremely dour with a piercing expression on his face, not easily amused, very demanding but very professional.

'During the time he had been running the team he had established administration procedures, a system of reports from drivers, technicians, the racing manager and the competitions secretary. Every race was analysed, any equipment failure was noted, expense details were listed, and driver performance was recorded. These were written out and distributed after every race meeting. They were extremely detailed and well put together and this was a process I had to continue. The man who had done the job before me was Peter Miller (a well-known journalist and motor racing personality at that time), but when I came along for a lot less money I did all these jobs as well as being secretary to Reg and to Roy Parnell, Reg's nephew.

'My enormous salary was £7 10s a week, and I remember at the end of my first year nervously making the request that perhaps there could be an increase. The answer was no, as I was earning more than any other woman in the company, but they gave me an end-of-year bonus of £25. So I continued at £7 10s a week despite the fact that I was

handling a great deal of money, working extraordinarily long hours
and most weekends – it was a sensitive point!

'Although John Wyer was no longer the racing manager, he
obviously kept in very close touch with everything that was being
done, and his technical knowledge was superb – he truly was an
amazing man. I got to know him better much later when my husband
Bib (Australian racing driver Bib Stillwell) and I lived in Tucson,
Arizona, and John and his wife Tottie had retired to Phoenix, mainly
due to his health. Tottie is a most amusing and amazing woman, and
to talk with her about John made me realise that she did not have an
easy time; he could be so down-putting, demanding and scathing
about people. But also she knew that she was with a man who could
be very sensitive and was basically insecure. A lot of the coldness we
saw was a front that he used to protect himself.'

'Reg was very popular and often very generous. As a gift at
Christmas time he would bring a choice hunk of pork for all the
mechanics and each member of staff in the racing department. As he
did not spend all his time at Hanworth Park, but commuted back and
forward to Derbyshire, the day-to-day running was in the hands of his
nephew Roy, who was also the chief test driver. When Reg was in
town he normally stayed at the Headfort Place Hotel in London,
which was another haunt of racing drivers as it was owned by John
Morgan, General Secretary of the BARC.'

When it came to race planning Gillian and Roy would sit down and
work out all the details for the transportation of cars, spare parts,
equipment, support vehicles and personnel – the scale of the
operation would depend on the race concerned. Le Mans was the
number one event, and was a major exercise. For a three-car entry the
team was expanded to perhaps 50 people, which included drivers,
mechanics, technicians, pit personnel, wives and girlfriends, and in
those days they were all expected to muck in as timekeepers, 'gofers'
and the like. Catering was supplied by Joe Walsham, a friend of Reg's
from Derby, who provided marvellous cuisine.

1959 was the big year for Aston Martin, and among the supporters
at Le Mans were two Americans from Chattanooga, Tennessee,
Josephus Conn Guild and Frank Harrison, who had been enthusiastic
followers of Aston Martin at the Sebring races. Both were highly
successful and wealthy businessmen, Jo in the electricity business and
Frank with a trucking company and a glass manufacturing business
that made bottles for Coca Cola. Frank had also run a car in the
Indianapolis 500 for Lloyd Ruby.

When they came over for the 24-hour race Jo hired a rental car complete with a French driver, and when everyone left the team headquarters at La Chartre-sur-le-Loir to travel in convoy to the circuit, the team used to get well ahead of Jo whose French driver was very careful on the road. Jo would then take out some French banknotes, tear them in two and give the chauffeur half, promising him the other half if he caught up with the cars ahead!

While motor racing was taken seriously in those days, at the same time the occasional party for the team after a race was always a break from the normal stresses and strains. After the 1957 Le Mans race, when the Aston Martins did not finish, Gillian remembers a particular party at the Cheval Blanc restaurant in La Chartre.

'I was wearing a dress with a slightly scooped back and as Reg walked past me he poured some Coca Cola down my back so I decided to retaliate. Reg by this time had twigged and pulled a raincoat over himself, but Eric Thomson, Pat Griffith and Gerald Lascelles decided to help and pulled up one of the sleeves of the raincoat and poured the Coca Cola down it. No one was in any way incapable – just having a bit of fun.

'In this happy state it was then decided to hold a competition. Two glasses of wine were placed at the end of a table and two people lined up at the other end. At the signal they had to run to the table, drink the wine and run back – they were timed to find the winner. Someone managed to persuade John Wyer to have a go. Now normally John would stand in a corner with a dark expression on his face, but this time he decided to join in. He rushed to get the glass of wine, slipped on the soaking floor and fell flat on his back. Well, there was a ghastly silence and we all expected him to be very annoyed and rip into everyone, but he got full marks by getting up, drinking the wine and running back again. It made the evening!'

As mentioned earlier, the logistics for race meetings were often immensely complicated, and when it came to strategy planning meetings John Wyer was always included, and he usually attended the races, but always stayed in the background.

In those days Aston Martin had a big truck that carried all the cars and a second smaller one that the mechanics used to call the 'Van Ordinaire'. For Le Mans the mechanics would drive the trucks and cross by ferry from Dover while the drivers and team personnel would fly from Lydd to Le Touquet on one of the two air ferries that used to carry private cars. Gillian remembers that 'we always had a little champagne party at Le Touquet before we set off to drive for La Chartre-sur-le-Loir.'

There was also the matter of driver contracts, and Gillian recalls an approach made by Aston Martin to Dan Gurney to drive. 'He replied saying he wanted a £5,000 retaining fee and we all thought it was absolutely hysterical as nobody had ever been paid that kind of money – so he didn't get a drive. Things have certainly changed when you think about the amounts paid to Michael Schumacher and the like today.'

By now Roy Salvadori was a long-serving team member, and when Reg took over as team manager Roy found a new problem. 'He ran the team on exactly the same lines as John Wyer, but at the meetings he always seemed to take it out on his old buddies. If anyone was going to get a bollocking it would be me, or if he had a hard job to do that nobody else wanted it always ended up with me. I had noticed when I first joined the team that Reg would always favour the newcomers, and he was the same as team manager. I found out later, once I became the regular driver, that it was as though Reg knew he could rely on you to do exactly what he wanted. If anything difficult came up he always gave the newcomer the easy option and I got the dirty work to do.

'It was the same when I drove for him years later in the Bowmaker team in the Tasman Series. On one occasion Jo Bonnier was brought into the team for the first time. The cars were a Lotus and a Cooper and we both wanted to drive the Cooper because the Lotus was notoriously unreliable. Reg not only gave the Cooper to Jo – who was only a guest driver for two races – but then told me to let Jo Bonnier win! I had no practice in the Lotus because the gearbox was in pieces and I was furious. I said to him, "Reg, what the hell are you playing at? I am your regular driver and you have a newcomer here demanding that he win the race and I place second." The next thing I knew the deal was we would share the starting and prize money, but a later amendment to this was that if I didn't finish I got virtually bugger all because the Lotus was so unreliable.

'We went into the race and I poured away from Bonnier to a 15-second lead, then I received the sign that virtually said "Let Bonnier past". I didn't know what to do and thought here's my old mate Reg and I cannot believe he is doing this to me. So I slowed down going past the pits to make it obvious to everybody that it was a fix. I gave Reg the two fingers then followed Bonnier over the line just to make sure everyone knew the score. Now that was old Reg – if he knew you, you could almost think he would take advantage of you.'

Reg could not have chosen a harder season than 1957 to launch his new career at Aston Martin. Behind the scenes the DBR1, the new sports car that had done so well at Le Mans the previous year, now had its capacity raised to 3 litres, and the team was given a tremendous boost when Tony Brooks and Roy Salvadori romped home first and second in a non-championship sports car race held at Spa. Hopes were therefore high for their first full World Championship event at the 1,000 kms at Nurburgring.

In those days the World Sports Car Championship was much more important to manufacturers than the Group C Championship of the 1980s, for instance. Maserati were desperate to win the Championship as money was tight, and to be World Champion of Makes would throw them a lifeline. As a result they developed their impressive and powerful 4.5 litre Maserati 450S sports car. To counter this Ferrari had various versions of their Testa Rossa, including a 4.1 litre V12.

As for the British, Jaguar had withdrawn as a factory team but assisted their private entrants and had a 3.8 litre six-cylinder engine to take the place of the normal 3.4. Aston Martin were virtually out of the World Championship as they had missed some of the early races, and such races as they did enter with the DBR1 were in preparation for a full assault in 1958.

Clearly the 1957 1,000 kms race at the Nurburgring was going to be a tough one. This hazardous and punishing circuit was not kind to cars or drivers, and this was going to be a real test as the bumps and twists of the Eiffel circuit would certainly winkle out any problems in the design of the car. To everyone's surprise, and perhaps utter shock within the Ferrari and Maserati camps, Tony Brooks and newcomer Noel Cunningham Reid romped home for a superb victory, having led the race for 42 of the 44 laps of this tortuous circuit. Not only that, but their winning speed was more than 10 minutes faster than Moss and Behra had recorded the previous year in a 3 litre Maserati.

Now it was full steam ahead for the Le Mans 24-hour race, where the team had three cars entered for Tony Brooks/Noel Cunningham Reid, Roy Salvadori/Les Leston and Graham and Peter Whitehead. The first two were regular 3 litre DBR1s, while the Whitehead car had been re-designed with a different chassis and was fitted with an experimental 3.7 litre engine, thus becoming the prototype DBR2. The bigger engine was felt necessary to give Astons that extra punch down the long Mulsanne Straight, but as it turned out the engine needed much more development time as the car was actually slower on lap times and, more significantly, slower on the Mulsanne Straight than the regular 3 litre cars! Almost predictably the car retired after eight hours when the engine expired. Two hours later the Salvadori car went out with a broken gearbox. The Brooks car was lying in second place behind the eventual winning car, the Ecurie Ecosse D type Jaguar of Flockhart and Ivor Bueb, when Brooks too began to have gearbox trouble.

'Noel Cunningham Reid, my co-driver, brought the car into the pits about four in the morning with it stuck in fourth gear. Now I had experienced this problem before at Spa. I had managed to get it out of fourth and win that race, so as we were in second place at Le Mans I didn't fancy running round for the next 12 hours in fourth gear dropping slowly down the field. Second was a good placing for an Aston in those days because it never had enough power on the long straight and the car excelled in its road holding. As soon as I got in the car I managed to get it away in fourth gear and took the long right-hander after the pits and the Esses, then going towards Tertre Rouge I did what you are told not to do when you are sitting your driving test and that is not to look down at the gear lever. So I was looking down at the gear lever, accelerating, pushing the clutch down and trying one of the tricks I had tried at Spa. Then I looked up suddenly and realised I was past my braking point. Absolute stupidity, and the thing was if I had been deeper into the corner it would have been better. I put the car sideways and I almost made it round the corner but there was a sandbank on the outside of the corner neatly chamfered, so when I came round the corner I still had a fair bit of forward motion, started running up the bank and the car just flipped over and trapped me underneath. That was bad enough, but I was far enough round the corner for my car not to be seen so I was lying there trapped under the car waiting to be run over or for it to catch fire.

'The next man round was Umberto Maglioli in a Porsche, and as I always say the guy was a gentleman because he ran wide and hit the car and knocked it off me so I got up a bit sharpish and hopped over the fence. I had suffered some pretty severe lacerations and to this day I have a hole in my side you could almost get your fist into. That was the reason why at my next race at Aintree – the British Grand Prix – I got out of my sickbed to go and practice the Vanwall, and although I managed to get the car on the front row of the grid I wasn't fit to run the full race. So that is why we agreed that if Stirling had trouble with his Vanwall in the race he would take over my car, and in fact that is what happened, which was just as well as I was not fit enough to actually finish the race.'

Aston Martin missed the Swedish and Venezuelan events in the World Championship but had the satisfaction of seeing Brooks win again in Belgium in the Grand Prix at Spa, which that year was made a sports car event.

Towards the end of 1957 the prototype of the DBR4/250 Formula 1 car was finally completed and Roy Salvadori and Reg took it to the industry test track at MIRA alongside the DBR1; however, the GP car project was put aside yet again while the company concentrated on winning the elusive World Sports Car Championship. The DBR1 proved its worth as a challenger during the 1958 Championship by setting up new lap records on the Targa Florio and winning both the Nurburgring 1000 kms for a second year running and the Tourist Trophy; but the Championship again went to Ferrari, partly because Aston Martin had a debacle at Le Mans where Ferrari won, and did not take part in the 1,000 kms race in the Argentine that opened the season, and in which Ferrari took first and second. There was talk that Aston Martin had not received the necessary forms in time to enter, but as it took place at the end of January 1958 they probably would not have been able to prepare a challenge anyway.

The cars were ready for Sebring, however, and two DBR1s were sent out with Stirling Moss and Tony Brooks sharing the car that Brooks had used to win Nurburgring the previous year, and Roy Salvadori sharing with American Carroll Shelby. Shelby was a great admirer of Reg; he had total faith in him as a team manager and respect for his former racing career.

Maserati were not at Sebring, still recovering from their humiliating defeat at the hands of Ferrari in the final round of the previous year's Championship, and the Jaguars and Lister-Jaguars were suffering from having to use 3 litre engines rather than their more familiar and reliable 3.4s and 3.8s. Ferrari, however, arrived in great strength with four factory cars and another three well-qualified private entries to back them up.

In practice Moss left everyone standing, and in the race sped off into the distance, holding the lead for four hours. By comparison with race performances today, Moss's drive in the opening hours of Sebring was nothing short of brilliant. At the end of the first hour he had lapped every car but nine of the 65-car field and had a lead of a minute and a half over his team mate Salvadori in the other Aston Martin! At a time when the Ferraris were all-powerful, the Astons were looking good, and Reg must have been feeling pleased with his first year's work. But then the trouble started.

Moss burst a tyre and had to run slowly round to the pits to change the wheel, but he still had a 50-second lead when he came out again. Carroll Shelby, however, had to retire the other Aston Martin when the transmission failed. When Tony Brooks took over the Moss car he was still leading Phil Hill's Ferrari, both of them now having lapped the entire field. But the red tide was building up behind them – Wolfgang Von Trips, Richie Ginther and Luigi Musso in three other factory Ferraris were holding third, fourth and fifth places. Then

Brooks was seen to have trouble changing gear, and when Collins took over the Hill Ferrari he was suddenly up behind Brooks. A quick pit stop to investigate saw Moss back in the car, but by now the Aston was over 3 minutes behind the Collins/Hill Ferrari. He went out and threw caution to the wind, bringing the Ferrari lead down to just 12 seconds, despite the bonnet flying off, chipping an edge off the windscreen and scoring Moss's visor!

However, the gearbox was now giving trouble and the car pulled in to retire from the race. Ironically, despite the fact that the Collins/Hill car was to win, Collins had warped the drums of the Ferrari's brakes and the agitated Hill kept telling team manager Tavoni to slow down Von Trips in the other Ferrari who was threatening them.

Again it was bitter disappointment, and again it was problems with the gearbox, which always seemed to be the fragile part of Aston Martins, but as the team was owned by the company that made the gearboxes Reg was in a difficult position. (As we will see later, he did fit a Maserati gearbox to a DBR1 to see if it made a difference.)

With orders to win the World Sports Car Championship, Reg had a few weeks to prepare for a really tough event, the Targa Florio. This open-road race had not been affected by the aftermath of the dreadful accident on the Mille Miglia in 1957, when Alfonso De Portago and his co-driver and many spectators had been killed. While open-road racing was banned in Italy, this was Sicily, and the race went on. With a single lap distance of 45 miles, it made circuits like the Nurburgring pale into insignificance. It also had ditches, changing surfaces, the odd animal and the spectators, who crowded every turn and made life decidedly difficult. It was a race for drivers who were at home on open roads, and with his Mille Miglia win in 1955 none could be more suited than Stirling Moss.

Reg fielded just one car for Moss and Tony Brooks against the might of Ferrari, but in Moss he held the trump card. The race was run with the cars setting off at intervals, as was the case with the Mille Miglia, so each driver was racing against the clock and was out to pass the man in front. Moss set off at high speed, but on his first lap he had the misfortune to clip a kilometre stone with his wheel when making a bold overtaking move on a slower car. He stopped at the end of the lap to change wheels and repair some other damage to the car, which took half an hour! Anyone who knows Stirling Moss will know that he never stopped trying, so when he jumped into the car he was ready for the challenge. On his first lap he promptly reeled off a new lap record, then took another 2 seconds off the record on his next. Ironically, he himself actually held the lap record for the course, set two years before in a Mercedes-Benz 300SLR. By the fourth lap he was back up to eighth place, but a lap later the car was out. Again the gearbox had let them down, and poor Brooks never even got a drive.

Recalling that race today and reacting to the comment that perhaps the Aston Martin DBR1 was not the best car for the Targa Florio, Brooks remarked, 'Well it was a pretty tough car and it was the gearbox that was the only really weak aspect of it. It was a great road-holding car and I don't think there was any problem about the ruggedness of the car on the Targa Florio apart from the gearbox. I think it was a very good car for the Targa.'

It was a lonely and sad trip back to England, and there was precious little time to prepare for the Nurburgring 1,000 kms race some 20 days later. The Championship year was well advanced and Ferrari had 10 points – Aston Martin had none.

For Nurburgring Reg decided to go the whole hog and run three cars, bringing two new drivers into the team. One was a member of the successful Vanwall team, Stuart Lewis Evans, and the other a man who was to go on to win two World Drivers Championships, Jack Brabham. He was not quite so famous then, and in the long and tiring race Stirling Moss, his driving partner, drove one of those races that must rate among the greatest of his career. He not only won, but his race average was a new record, he broke the lap record twice and drove for nearly 6 hours of the race's 7 hrs 20 mins.

Ferrari were again out in force, but at the start of the race Moss flew off with Brooks and Salvadori in second and third. Mike Hawthorn in his Ferrari elbowed his way into second place by the end of the first lap, but already Moss had a 12-second lead and was to take a full 7 seconds off the lap record on his second lap. Brooks spun his Aston Martin at the Karussel, and Roy Salvadori brought the third Aston Martin into the pits early in the race with the gearbox selector doing strange things – and Nurburgring was the last circuit where a driver wanted a troublesome gearbox. Then Tony Brooks got caught up in one of those situations that used to happen in long-distance races at Nurburgring in those days. There was usually a huge and varied entry and the standards of driving ranged from World Championship to retarded Club racer. Tony Brooks recalls what happened to him.

'I remember I was on one of the very fast downhill sections of the Ring and can visualise it even now with a gentle long right-hander coming up followed by a left-hand. This Peugeot – I even remember what car it was, which is highly unusual for me – was on the left of the road and apparently had seen me but he should really have been on the right. He was hugging the left so I thought he wanted to hold his line. I started to go round the outside of him and you must remember we were knocking on a bit. I must have been doing 140-150 mph rushing downhill, and this guy started to move slowly over and over to my side of the road and I finished up in the ditch, which fortunately was all chamfered away. There aren't many ditches you can afford to go off into at the Ring, but this was one of them. He just drove me off the road and had to be totally unaware of me as he would have been a lunatic to deliberately try to do it. If I had held my ground I would have caused the most monumental accident, and although I would have been all right he would have had a few problems. So I moved over and finished up on the grass in the ditch, and it was impossible to get the car out.'

At the first pit stop Moss handed over to Brabham, but the lead he had built up was scythed away by Hawthorn. This was too much, so Brabham was hauled back in after only two laps and Moss jumped into the car and set about doing the business again. After 24 laps Moss came back into the pits with a 2½-minute lead, but Brabham then lost time to Collins, and four laps later he was called back in again and Moss took over once more. Although Reg's timekeepers noticed that Moss appeared to have slowed on one lap, he still charged on and won the race.

It was only afterwards, at the Aston Martin briefing, that Moss admitted that on the lap during which the timekeepers had noticed a difference in his times he had actually spun the car, but had not hit anything; for once luck was with him and with Aston Martin.

The pressure was now on and three cars were prepared for Le Mans, where again they were looking good. Moss, master of the Le Mans starts, sprinted away from everyone leaving team mate Tony Brooks to deal with the Ferraris of Hawthorn and Von Trips. But once again it was not to last, and when Moss's engine dropped to five cylinders the writing was on the wall and he was out of the race within just three hours. But there were more disasters to come as the heavens opened and the rain poured down, catching out poor Lewis Evans who lost his Aston around the Dunlop bridge and crashed out of contention. The Trintignant/Brooks car soldiered on and was holding a steady third place behind the Gendebien/Hill Ferrari and the remarkable Duncan Hamilton/Ivor Bueb D type Jaguar when the transmission again let them down and the last Aston Martin went out of the race. Ferrari took the points yet again.

With only one race to go in the Championship, Ferrari had it in the bag. However, they did not turn up for the 1958 Tourist Trophy race at Goodwood, which saw Aston Martin out in force, so it was virtually a British National race meeting with the three Aston Martins virtually unchallenged and finishing first, second and third. But although Aston Martin had gone out of the 1958 season with a bang, Reg knew in his heart that it was a hollow victory and that they had to get back to work and make sure things went right in 1959.

Around this time the company launched the Aston Martin DB4 and John Wyer thought up the idea of some kind of record suggesting that the car could accelerate to 100 mph and stop again in less than 30 seconds. Alan Dakers, their public relations officer at the time, soon to go to Renault, thought that this was a good idea, but clearly they had to prove it could be done. It was decided that Reg's nephew Roy should be entrusted with the job, and the car was taken to the MIRA facility where it was officially observed. In fact the DB4 managed 0 to 100 mph and back to 0 in just 27 seconds, and so the car was launched with this little gem of information.

At the end of 1958 Mike Hawthorn was crowned World Drivers' Champion, and Reg had a relaxing night out at the Daily Express Sports Personality of the Year dinner, sitting at the same table as Hawthorn, Tony Vandervell and Britain's most successful motor cycle rider, John Surtees. Remembering this dinner, Surtees comments: 'At that dinner they all started talking to me about trying cars and Reg said, "I must give you a test in an Aston Martin." Then Tony Vandervell said, "No he won't, he's a motorcyclist like me – if he's going to drive he'll drive one of my Vanwalls and not one of those – he didn't use a very complimentary word about David Brown – things." Then Mike chipped in and agreed with them.'

The conversation was convivial, and as a result they all agreed to meet up again at the BBC Sportsview Personality of the Year dinner some weeks later. Sadly in the meantime Mike Hawthorn was killed in a road accident, and it was almost a year before Reg, true to his word, rang Surtees and reminded him of the conversation.

Chapter 11

1959: Final Assault On Le Mans

IN APRIL 1959 Aston Martin called a press conference to announce their worst-kept secret, namely that they had developed a grand prix car. The drivers were to be Roy Salvadori and Carroll Shelby.

Recalling the DBR4/250 he had tested back in December 1957, Salvadori remarked 'At that time (1957), in my opinion, it would have been practically unbeatable. By 1959 it was still a good car with good road-holding and brakes, but it didn't have much power.

'We had a problem in our first race at Silverstone, the Daily Express Trophy in 1959. Although I finished second to Jack Brabham, it was only a 140-mile race as opposed to a grand prix distance of about 300 miles. The engines used by Carroll and I were totally clapped out and we had to reduce our revs in the race from around 7,500 to about 7,000, which gave us a very narrow band of power. At Aintree in the British Grand Prix the car still felt reasonably competitive thanks to its road-holding and brakes, but we were again using 7,300-7,500 revs in practice.

'Remember that the cars had never run in a full grand prix because back in those days you never did a full test run over a grand prix distance. It was all very well stopping and starting, and miles could have added up, but as soon as we started to do a full grand prix we were in trouble, plus the fact that the gearbox was a pig. Throughout that year we seemed to go backwards even though, basically, the car was super. If you had put a Maserati or a Ferrari engine into it, it would have been unbeatable.

'Typically, over the next year Reg oversaw the design of a completely new and lighter car with independent suspension, when we should have been working on the weight, the engine and the gearbox of the existing car.'

After a lot of discussion it was agreed that the programme would be turned on its head and Aston Martin would concentrate on the Formula 1 car and put all their sports car eggs into winning Le Mans, as it was going to be their tenth effort.

Clearly Reg was keen to get ahead with the grand prix car because his interests had always lain with grand prix cars, and following his own underfinanced efforts with the Challenger, he now had a chance to develop a race-winning car. The fact that the DBR4 was a front-engined car at a time when the trends were pointing to rear-engined designs was not initially seen as a problem. In answer to a journalist's question about the position of the engine, John Wyer remarked sarcastically, 'Well, the car doesn't know where the engine is, does it?'

The best-laid plans can often be changed by the most unlikely circumstances, and when Sebring race organiser Alec Ullmann pleaded with Reg and John Wyer to enter a car for the race, which was the first round in the World Sports Car Championship, and as an added incentive offered to pay the entire expenses for one car to go, it was an offer they couldn't refuse. So the 1959 Sports Car Championship was fought out by two battered old warriors, Aston Martin with their now ageing DBR1 3000 and Ferrari with their even older Testa Rossa derivatives, plus a new upstart called Porsche.

It is difficult to appreciate at this distance in time that whereas Jaguar and Aston Martin had been using disc brakes for years, the Ferraris were still using drum brakes on their sports cars. But this changed for 1959 when all their cars were finally modified to discs, despite all of Enzo Ferrari's claims that drum brakes were still efficient.

Although Porsche had been competing in world-class sports car racing since the early 111950s, they had always run in the lower capacity classes, usually winning thanks to their reliability. The stylish 550 Spyder had given way to the RSK 1500, and it became clear that on the tight and twisty circuits they were nimble enough to give the bigger cars a run for their money. This was just the beginning of Porshe's eventual domination of sports car racing in the 1970s and the '80s.

Five events counted for the Championship, all of them the big show events – Sebring, Targa Florio, Nurburgring 1,000 kms, Le Mans and the Tourist Trophy. Of these Aston Martin had already triumphed at Nurburgring and Goodwood, and the key to success was truly Le Mans; Aston Martin had to win Le Mans to have any chance. Le Mans was also the race that David Brown had dreamed of winning. It held a great cachet in terms of production car sales, as Jaguar and Ferrari had previously demonstrated, and this was Aston Martin's first year with the DB4.

The trouble was that sports car racing of this type was really dying, although those of us wrapped up in it did not fully appreciate this. When a GT car finish third overall at Le Mans, it made people sit up and take notice and wonder where this sports car formula was going.

David Brown had hinted that this would possibly be Aston Martin's last season in sports car racing, and this was in fact what happened – but in much happier circumstances than had been envisaged at the start of the season.

By now Reg had no excuses and he really had to shape up and produce the goods. However, the troublesome gearbox that had dogged Aston Martin in the past still appeared to be the weak link in the chain, and Sebring was to underline this once again.

For the first round at Sebring only one car was sent out with Carroll Shelby and Roy Salvadori at the wheel, Stirling Moss having agreed to drive a Lister-Jaguar. It was Salvadori who took the first stint at the wheel; he did what Moss had done the previous year and led at the end of the first lap, with Dan Gurney's Ferrari breathing down his neck. The car lasted only 3½ of the 12 hours, and retired with various transmission problems including a broken clutch. Zero points. Ferrari finished first and second, and Porsche, the upstarts, took the next three places.

The Targa Florio was never going to be considered, nor was Nurburgring until Stirling Moss stepped in. As the Porsches had totally swept the board in the Sicilian event by taking the first four places, Ferrari were denied further points. Although Stirling Moss has always had the reputation of thinking of money first, he surprised everyone by telephoning John Wyer and asking him if he could be loaned a DBR1 for the 1,000 kms event, as he felt confident that it was a winner. He knew that Aston Martin were only interested in Le Mans, so he offered to pay for all the expenses out of his own pocket. However, it was decided that Reg and a couple of mechanics would go along at Aston's expense to help him. The car he was given was exactly the same car as he had used to win in 1956.

After practice Moss asked Reg for a lower gear ratio, which was strange because the old Nurburgring circuit was not only famous for its many corners but for a particularly long straight. Reg was worried that Stirling might then over-rev the car on the straight, but he knew that Moss did not make judgements without a great deal of thought and agreed to lower the ratio.

Moss was in magical form once again and completely dominated the race from start to finish, even breaking his own lap record three times. In the opening 17 laps he opened out a lead of nearly 5½ minutes over the rest of the field before handing over to co-driver Jack Fairman. Then the fun and the rain started. Fairman started to lose time to the hard-charging Jean Behra in his Ferrari, then to make matters worse he spun the Aston off the road and into a ditch. It is not hard to imagine Stirling Moss's feelings and his mood in the pits when the news came through. Normally if you went off into a ditch at Nurburgring you were finished, but Fairman hauled a fence-post out of the ground and managed to cajole the car back on to the road and back to the pits, but by then two of the Ferraris and the brilliant Umberto Maglioli in his Porsche had flashed past. Moss got back into the Aston Martin and proved once again what a truly great racing driver he was by catching the Porsche and Gendebien's Ferrari within four laps. He then had good fortune with the Ferrari's scheduled pit stops, which put him back into the lead again. He pulled out another lead of 1 min 43 secs, then called into the pits to hand over to Fairman again. Once more Fairman was caught, this time by Phil Hill's Ferrari, and Moss, furious, had him brought back into the pits for good. The rules of the race were such that Moss was not allowed to run the full event on his own and was obliged to hand over to the co-driver, but this time Moss already had a foot over the door as Fairman was trying to get out of the car. Back at the wheel Moss again did the impossible, catching Hill a few laps later on one of the most dangerous parts of the circuit, and from then on nothing, and certainly not Jack Fairman, was going to stop him winning the race.

Aston Martin now had 8 points in the Championship with two rounds to go. Porsche was leading with 15 points to Ferrari's 14, so a newcomer had entered into the battle.

Le Mans proved to be a tactical tour de force for Reg Parnell. For one thing he was very familiar with the Italians and knew how they thought and how agitated they could get if everything was not going their way. There was no doubt whatsoever that this race was to be Waterloo and Alamein rolled into one. The Ferrari team of three cars were strong and fast and were quickest on the track during practice. To back them up were four private 250GTs, all with top drivers at the wheel, and clearly Ferrari were out for bear in this race.

Reg fielded three factory Aston Martin DBR1s, and there was a factory-assisted private entry from Graham Whitehead and sports car driver Brian Naylor. And as if to cock a snook at the Ferrari 250GTs, there were also two Swiss private entrants with an Aston Martin DB4GT.

Reg's plan was to go out and try and force the Ferraris to set off at too fast a pace, one that they could not sustain. Towards this end the

Moss/Fairman Aston Martin had the more powerful four-bearing engine, while the Salvadori/Shelby and Trintignant/Frère cars had more conventional long-distance seven-bearing engines. The reasoning for this is explained by Salvadori: 'We all knew what the plan was, and if you think about it it was logical. With the four-bearing engine Stirling could go like hell and hope that the Ferraris would be led into the trap. Having driven both types of car I can tell you that with a thoroughbred race engine like a Ferrari you always had a lot of surplus revs in hand, which gives you much more leverage, whereas with an Aston you really had to stick to your revs if you wanted to finish. Then you must remember that the Ferrari team, with drivers like Jean Behra and Dan Gurney in it, was not too disciplined and not clever enough, otherwise they would have twigged what was going on and told their drivers to slow down.'

As usual Stirling Moss was across the track and away before anyone else, and at the end of the first lap was clearly in the lead. It was Nurburgring all over again and the Ferraris didn't like it. Jean Behra in particular didn't like it, and spurred on by his home crowd he weaved through the field and took the lead from Moss an hour after the start. During the first pit stops Reg, his familiar megaphone in his hands, could see that his strategy was working, for all three factory Ferraris came in at the same time, providing a bit of the familiar Chinese fire-drill that was a Ferrari pit stop.

When Fairman took the wheel Phil Hill began to threaten, but the first cross could be put on the Aston pit wall when Cliff Allison began to have trouble with his Ferrari and finally retired with a failed gearbox. One down. Then Phil Hill's Ferrari began to have trouble with the carburettors and dropped back.

By the seventh hour Moss's race was won, but the grand prix pace he had set in the warm conditions had red-ragged the Ferrari bull and they were to see the consequences as the race went on. Salvadori took the lead and held it for the next four hours before the hard-charging Gendebien/Phil Hill Ferrari went past into the lead. Salvadori had a problem with vibration and came into the pits, but Reg sent him out again to do another few laps so that they would fall into the 30-lap window before refuelling the car. This slowed the car down somewhat, and Salvadori had some catching up to do.

Henry Taylor recalls being in the Aston Martin pits at this time and describes Salvadori's plight: 'Something went wrong when Roy was driving and it was not easy to find out what was wrong. He said, "I can't steer it", went out again, came back again and they couldn't find anything, did one lap and said he didn't know what was wrong. So Reg said, "Get out the f---ing car" and he jumped into it and told the mechanics to jack up the back end. He put it in fourth gear and spun the wheels and immediately the car nearly fell off the jack because half the tread was missing on one of the tyres – so Reg had literally solved the problem in ten seconds.'

Tim Parnell remembers some other background incidents with the *plombier*. This was the official from the Automobile Club who supervised every fuel stop, snipped the seals to enable the car to refuel, then resealed the fuel filler cap afterwards.

'I was refuelling the cars and as the race went on our *plombier* got into a dreadful state. Every time one of our cars came in I had to get him out of his little hut, and every time I went in he was drinking more and more wine and I ended up more or less carrying him to the car to cut the seals off, fill the car up, get him to seal the car up, then carry him back to his little shed.'

As anyone who has been at Le Mans knows, the race begins to atrophy during the morning as everyone decides to consolidate positions and simply hack it out to the end. This was a period of great tension at Aston Martin; they were well placed, but history advised them to just hang on in there come what may.

At 11 am the leading Ferrari suddenly arrived in the pits with steam everywhere. The Ferrari mechanics tried everything they knew to stop the water leak, but within a few laps it was out. Even the Porsches were suffering, so with some four hours to go Roy Salvadori and Carroll Shelby took over the lead in their Aston Martin followed by Maurice Trintignant and Paul Frère in their sister car and they held their places right to the end, the second place car being nearly 200 miles ahead of the third-placed Ferrari GT of Beurlys and Helde. Indeed, the third to sixth positions were taken by three Ferrari 250GTs and a California Spyder; this pointed to the emerging importance of this particular class, which was not overlooked by Reg who was already thinking about the new DB4.

Towards the end of the race there was a little incident in the pits that was very rare. The Astons were lying first and second, and John Wyer felt that if the second car were speeded up it would help break some record that nobody can recall today. Reg objected to this idea and he and Wyer had a slightly heated confrontation, Reg pointing out that Aston Martin were trying to finish this race in first and second places. The second car was already awash in oil and had other problems, and he felt that they could not take the risk of speeding it up. On this occasion Reg won the day, but Gillian Harris adds that there were other occasions when John Wyer made decisions that Reg

resented and to which he objected. It must be remembered that these
were the days when Jaguar appeared to be kings and there was a lot of
pressure from David Brown for Aston Martin to knock them off their
throne.

When the race ended the entire Aston Martin team, from the most
lowly mechanic to David Brown himself, breathed a collective sigh of
relief. At last they had won the race that they had battled ten years to
win. David Brown jumped on to the back of the car with Salvadori
and Moss on the way to scrutineering and was clearly delighted at the
result.

John Wyer was also pleased with the work that Reg had done and
reported that 'Reg Parnell's control of the race was superb and the
battle was always being fought on his terms. By contrast Ferrari
allowed themselves to fall into the elementary trap of being drawn
into the fight too soon by Stirling's self-sacrificing performance in the
first two hours.'

After all the excitement and celebrations at the circuit, Reg turned
to his secretary Gillian and suggested that a group of them should
head off for the team hotel at La Chartre. 'We climbed into the old
Lagonda shooting-brake and got caught up in all the heavy race
traffic. I remember Reg turning to me and saying, "You know . . .",
then promptly falling asleep without finishing the sentence.'

On the Monday after the race their American friend Jo Conn Guild
took David Brown, the drivers, Reg, wives, girlfriends, timekeepers,
etc., to a wonderful restaurant near Le Mans for a celebratory lunch.
They sat in a lovely courtyard, with an old, high stone wall shining
white in the sunshine. Jo stood up and gave a speech thanking
everyone for the opportunity he had had to share in this exciting
event, and that he was breaking his vow of abstinence after 12 years.
He proposed a toast to David Brown and the drivers, drained the last
drop of wonderful vintage wine, then threw his glass behind him to
shatter against the stone wall.

Now Reg was faced with a real problem. He was in the midst of the
DB4 grand prix programme and although they had abandoned the
idea of going for the World Sports Car Championship, here they were
with one race to go one point ahead of Porsche and only two points
behind Ferrari. The last round was Goodwood, and if they could win
that event they would win the Championship. In fact, if a Ferrari
finished second there would be a points tie, but Aston would take the
title due to their number of outright wins.

Aston Martin arrived at Goodwood with something that made
everyone sit up and take notice – air jacks. I remember at this

particular race walking up to the Aston Martin DBRs and seeing these little valve holes on the wings and wondering what they were. To make the maximum publicity out of this, Aston Martin put on a demonstration for the press before practice, with Roy Parnell doing a dummy pit stop. The idea had been copied from the Indianapolis cars, and the team had lines from air bottles in the pits that were connected to these wing nozzles and the four jacking legs shot out from under the car and raised it for wheel changing.

When the first day of practice was over the cars were parked in the open paddock behind the pits and one of the rival Porsche engineers was seen on his hands and knees looking closely under the wings. Reg strolled past with his hands in his pockets and casually remarked to the Porsche man, 'It's no bloody good looking at that now, it's too bloody late for you to do anything about it!'

For Aston Martin and Reg Parnell the TT was a home fixture on both the team's and Reg's favourite circuit, Goodwood. Ferrari and Porsche pulled out the stops and were there in force. The rest could almost be ignored – they were there just to fill up the entry list and, in the case of Masten Gregory with the Ecurie Ecosse Tojeiro-Jaguar, to provide some light relief. (Midway through the race Masten left his braking too late at Woodcote and pulled off the remarkable trick of jumping up on to the seat so that when the car plummeted into the earth bank at high speed he was thrown high into the air and suffered relatively light injuries. This not only surprised Olivier Gendebien, who was overtaken by the wayward Tojeiro, and 'could not believe my eyes when I saw Masten crouched on the seat as he shot past me into the banking', but also annoyed his co-driver, a youthful Jim Clark, in his one and only race for Ecurie Ecosse.)

This was just one element in the Hollywood drama that was to unfold. Picture the scene – Stirling Moss rushes to his car and takes the lead from the Le Mans start with Shelby tucked in behind. But wait, Graham Hill hasn't read the script and has his 2 litre Lotus in third place. The Ferraris meanwhile have started off slowly and will lose Phil Hill early on when his engine breaks a rocker. Dan Gurney, however, is hurling his 3 litre Ferrari round the circuit as though it is a toy, smoking tyres, lots of arm movements, real motor racing. He closes on Carroll Shelby, but team mate Tony Brooks cannot give him much support as he is having trouble with his brakes, and team manager Romolo Tavoni is sceptical until one of the marshals hands in some bits of brake that prove that Brooks is right.

Cut to the chase – Salvadori is now driving the leading Aston Martin and comes into the pits for a routine fuel and tyres pit stop.

The refueller rushes forward with the fuel pipe but turns the tap a fraction of a second too soon and petrol floods down the sculpted rear wings of the car, hits the exhaust pipe and everything goes up in flames, the car, the pipe, the tank in the pit and a stretch of the wooden pits. It is the DB3 incident of a few years before repeated. Luckily this time there are no serious injuries but the car is out – to be later rebuilt and sold to Border Reivers for Jim Clark. (At Le Mans the following year Clark and Salvadori finished third in this car, the highest placed British entry.)

The script is immediately re-written. The luckless Jack Fairman – who has had a grass-cutting exercise earlier in the race – is brought in and Moss jumps into the car and proceeds to do a 'Stirling', rushing up through the field and passing back markers on his way to the front again. The Aston pits, however, are a shambles, the wooden structure totally burned out. To his credit private entrant Graham Whitehead withdraws his Aston Martin from the race so that Reg and his team can take over his pit.

This is no normal finish to a World Championship, this is a Hollywood movie of epic proportions. Out on the track it is not a Ferrari in the lead but the Porsche of Jo Bonnier and Wolfgang von Trips, but they are not going to stop Moss. He is on a high and you just have to sit back and relish this man at the peak of his form. The drama is not yet over because a Porsche is now second and the third place Ferrari is being driven by a raft of Ferrari drivers, Olivier Gendebien, Phil Hill, Tony Brooks and Cliff Allison, desperate to catch and pass the Porsche and give Ferrari at least a tie in the Championship.

Plot change again – Gendebien in the Ferrari moves into second place but is flagged in and the car given to Tony Brooks, who goes out there and drives hard but, wait, something's wrong, he isn't catching the second-place Porsche. Back in the Ferrari pit someone points out to Tavoni that he keeps giving Brooks signals that he is second when in fact he is third. No! Yes! Chinese fire-drill again as the frantic signals go out to Brooks. Now Brooks has another problem, as he has come up behind Stirling Moss. Moss, in the lead, is a lap ahead and conveniently makes his Aston a little wider than usual as he well knows that if Brooks catches the Porsche, Aston Martin will only share the Championship. Eventually Brooks gets through and the finish is a grandstander with the silver Porsche crossing the line just 5 seconds ahead of the Ferrari.

So what had happened in the Ferrari pit? Brooks again: 'It was unbelievable. There is a photograph that shows the pit board I was shown and it gives the Porsche driver's name then plus two seconds.

Now I have always believed that if you were plus two seconds you were two seconds ahead, but they meant that the Porsche was two seconds ahead of me! I believe that where I am, I am either plus somebody or minus somebody, and they said afterwards that what made the difference was that they had added an arrow, but for goodness sake I had been looking at Ferrari signals all year, so how could I possibly get it wrong at that time unless they had changed something without telling me? I can honestly say that at that time I believed I was ahead, but in fact I was behind, and if I had caught that wretched Porsche we would have won the Sports Car Championship for Ferrari. It was rather an expensive mistake or misunderstanding.'

Aston Martin had won the Championship outright. After all those years it had happened and Reg got all the credit he deserved. In the early years Aston had not been fully competitive, but now they were and it had been expected of him to go out there and win, despite any weaknesses the car had, and he made it. It was probably the most satisfying victory of his life.

Almost by default the 1959 season had provided everything that David Brown had wished for – a win at the 24-hour race at Le Mans and the World Sports Car Championship. In the background was the Formula 1 car, which perhaps had not had the attention it deserved because of the change of plans, but this situation was to alter almost immediately.

At a celebration dinner in October 1959 David Brown announced that Aston Martin were withdrawing from sports car racing and in 1960 would concentrate on Formula 1. A year after their dinner conversation, Reg telephoned John Surtees and invited him down to Goodwood to try an Aston Martin. John asked if he could bring his MV Agusta team mate John Hartle with him, to which Reg agreed.

The invention of the computer transformed day-to-day pit work in motor racing, and it is often hard to remember how much of a chore the recording of information and competitors' times actually was. I am grateful to Reg's secretary of the time, Gillian Harris, for sending me her simple brown-covered students' notebook in which she wrote down all the details, not only at races but also at test sessions. It was all laboriously hand-written and was presumably then typed out as a report for later consumption and filing.

On 21 December 1959 is the entry relating to the first Surtees test session. Gillian wrote that the Aston Martin DBR1 was chassis 01 and that the engine was RB6 300/2. Surprisingly the car was fitted with a Maserati gearbox – surprisingly because David Brown, owner of Aston Martin, manufactured gearboxes – but clearly it was no secret as it is written in Gillian's book. It is also stated that the back axle ratio was 4.09:1 and the outside air temperature was a cool 47 degrees.

We read that Surtees went out and lapped steadily, getting down to a 1:37.2 before spinning off. After lunch he got down to 1:36.6, then changed tyres and recorded a 1:35.2, coming in and complaining about the tyres.

Later in the afternoon his friend John Hartle, a fellow motor cycle racer, went out in a racing car for the first time and spun off just a few laps later. The testing was then stopped.

John Surtees recollected that cold day: 'When I arrived Reg literally told me to get into the car and just get on with it. He came across as a fatherly type of figure and he told me a bit about the car and how it had been the car Stirling Moss had used to win the 1,000 kms at Nurburgring. He said that it was a bit different from their normal cars, but didn't say why. In fact, it had a Maserati gearbox that David Brown was not supposed to know about. I did a few laps and came in, then John Hartle had a few laps and he spun just before the chicane. When I got back into the car and did a few more laps I thought this could be quite good, but nobody said anything. Then Reg came up to me with a bit of paper and said, "You'd better sign this." So I said, "What's this?" and he said, "It's a contract . . . you've been quicker than Stirling so sign this." I told him I wasn't signing contracts as I was a motor cyclist and already tied up, but Reg said, "We'll bring a Formula 1 car down and you can try that."

'Well, shortly after I got home from Goodwood the phone rang and it was Tony Vandervell. "What the hell are you doing driving one of those bloody things – if you're going to drive any cars you're going to drive Vanwall. I'm sending down the Vanwalls for you. I've fixed it all up." Sure enough they brought the Vanwalls down to Goodwood with David York and of course again I was driving a car Stirling had been racing. So I went round and round Goodwood again. Tony was enthusiastic and told me he was going to build me a car. However, his secretary told me not to get Tony too excited as everyone was worried about his heart. He actually went out and bought a Lotus 18 (chassis 901) into which he put one of his converted Vanwall engines.'

The day after their first Aston Martin test, Surtees and Hartle were back at Goodwood with the same DBR1 using the same engine, and the weather was not much warmer. This was a short test session where Surtees spun at Madgwick during his 21 laps in the car, then Hartle went out and immediately spun at the chicane on the first lap. He spun again on the third lap and eventually got down to a time around 4 seconds slower than Surtees. It was then decided that Surtees should come back to Goodwood and test the Formula 1 car for the first time two weeks later, on 5 January 1960, during a test session arranged by Avon tyres; Roy Salvadori would be present to do the bulk of the testing and provide a comparison.

The Formula 1 car used was the original prototype, DBR4/1, with engine RB6 250/2. The circuit was damp and it was cold and windy. Within six laps Salvadori was down to 1.33 and eventually got down to 1.30.2 using an experimental set of tyres. Standard tyres were then put on the car and Surtees was allowed out, but after a few laps the throttle stuck open and he quickly pitted with the rev counter showing 8,600 rpm!

After lunch the sun came out but the track was still damp and Surtees was able to knock 5 seconds off his previous best time, recording a very respectable 1:33.6 before coming in and reporting that the brakes were juddering. Salvadori then took the car out and spun when braking for the chicane.

As the track was still damp a switch was made to rain tyres, and Salvadori did a 1:30.2 to Surtees's 1:32.2, so clearly John Surtees had great potential and Reg was keen to sign him.

Two weeks later another young driver came down to Goodwood from his farm in Scotland; his name was Jim Clark. He was given the same Aston Martin DBR1 that Surtees had used and the circuit conditions were described as 'damp – frost thawing'. Clark completed 17 laps in the car with two pit visits, and in that time got down to a respectable 1:32.4, 3 seconds a lap faster than Surtees had achieved on his first test. Then the grand prix car was rolled out, only this was DBR4/2 and he did 23 laps with his best time being 1:30.0. After lunch he continued with the car and eventually recorded 1:29.8. Again Reg was impressed and asked Clark to come back to Goodwood a fortnight later, when Clark and Salvadori could test together.

Talking about this particular test session, Clark told me that by then John Surtees had decided to sign for Vanwall and not Aston Martin, but Reg had promised to give John Hartle a second test, which was also arranged for that particular test day. Although Surtees never drove for Reg while he was with Aston Martin, Reg always carried a torch for him and predicted that he would be World Champion. As was to be proved many times over, Reg had a good eye for talent and their paths were to cross again some years later.

The sports car selected for Clark on this second test was the larger-engined DBR2/1, and Salvadori took it out to warm it up and check the handling. He did a 1:34.6, then Clark went out for four laps with a fastest of 1:37.0. He then handed the car over to John Hartle, who did ten laps and on the last managed 1:37.7, but then crashed badly just before Woodcote, stopping that test session after only 41 minutes of track time.

Salvadori and Clark continued testing with the Formula 1 grand prix car DBR4/2 while John Hartle went home. During the afternoon both Salvadori and Clark experimented with Dunlop tyres rather than Avons, and Clark was to record the fastest time of the day at 1:27.2. As a result Reg decided that he would sign Jim Clark to race alongside Roy Salvadori in the Aston Martin team in 1960.

Chapter 12

1960-1961:
Yeoman Service

LATE IN 1959 Reg Parnell had to make some decisions regarding the Aston Martin Formula 1 team for the following year. He had expected John Surtees to sign, but although it upset him when John decided to join Tony Vandervell to drive a new prototype Vanwall, Reg had great faith in Surtees and it was not to spoil their relationship.

Following his test drive the probability was that Jim Clark would be signed up to drive alongside Roy Salvadori. Indeed, Jim's friend and confidant Ian Scott Watson, who ran the Border Reivers racing team, was getting excited about this prospect and early in 1960 asked Aston Martin PR man Alan Dakers whether he could say anything about Clark's imminent signing, as he was being pressurised by the Scottish press. On 16 February Dakers replied that he would rather Scott Watson stalled the press by saying that Aston Martin would make an official announcement in the near future, and even urged Scott Watson to prevent anything being published in advance.

The problem was that Reg had to have a word with Jimmy's father, and in a letter to Scott Watson a few days later he wrote: 'I was sorry not to see you during my visit to Berwick. Matters were eventually resolved with Jimmy and his father – the latter is not really an easy person to deal with!'

Reg was at that time a Vice-President of the Border Motor Racing Club, which Scott Watson had formed (and which was later to take over the operations of the then dormant Scottish Motor Racing Club), and he commented that he felt guilty that he was unable to devote much time to club activities and offered to stand down if he could find someone able to support the club in a more satisfactory way. As it turned out he was to remain a Vice-President until a little later, when Jim Clark was made President; today Jackie Stewart holds that post, having taken over the reins on the death of Jim Clark.

While all this was going on, the Border Reivers, led by Scott Watson and Jock McBain, were negotiating to buy the Aston Martin DBR1/3 that had caught fire in the pits at Goodwood during the 1959 Tourist Trophy race, and a deal was finally agreed in March 1960.

McBain wrote to John Wyer with a cheque for £425, representing the 10% deposit on the car, and Wyer replied with a pro forma invoice confirming that the car would be delivered to the Reivers 'exactly similar to the cars driven by Moss and other drivers during 1958 and 1959'.

The deal included a variety of spare parts including a five-speed gearbox and final drive unit, and a complete set of gear ratios used by Astons over the whole period that they had been operating DBR1s. Wyer added: 'Although there are in theory 66 different ratios, in fact by no means all the gears to provide these ratios have ever been made.' There was also a spare set of four Borrani wheel rims, prop shaft and suspension arms, plus a complete extra-high tail for the car and the alternative exhaust system used at Le Mans. Wyer also wrote that 'we will supply a number of spare tappets but I would point out that we do not vary the valve clearance by the thickness of the tappet. In the racing cylinder head this is done entirely by the seating of the valve . . . we will also supply a set of pneumatic jacks ready to be fitted to the car, but with regard to the control valve we are obviously unable to give you a guarantee and it will be for you to make your own approach to I. V. Pressure Controllers Ltd, in Feltham, from whom we obtain the valves on loan.'

By this time McBain had already applied for an entry for Le Mans and had received rapid confirmation of this from the AC de L'Ouest, presumably because of the Reivers' good showing at their first Le Mans in 1959, when Clark and Whitmore had raced a Lotus Elite. McBain asked John Wyer about help with a co-driver for Clark, and Wyer replied, 'Our final point concerns the possibility that Salvadori should act as co-driver to Jim Clark at Le Mans. I have been in touch with Salvadori and he would be very happy to drive with Jim but on condition that you would also be prepared to enter the car for the 1,000 Kilometres race at the Nurburgring with himself as co-driver. This would seem to me to be an excellent arrangement, but no doubt you will consider the matter and let me know what you decide.'

Before the Le Mans race the organisers decided to introduce a new regulation that went against the rules of Appendix C of the International Code. They insisted on windscreens being made of laminated glass at a time when the majority of sports cars had Perspex screens. Reg wrote to Raymond Acat at the AC de L'Ouest in the strongest terms: 'Entrants will now have to design, build and fit a glass screen in the very short time between the present date (6 May) and the Le Mans race (June). This modification would entail great expense and, more important, we feel that it would be impossible to carry out the work in the limited time.'

Salvadori and Clark did share the Reivers car and they went on to finish third at Le Mans, winning the *Motor* Trophy for the best-placed British car at the event.

In a letter to Scott Watson afterwards, Salvadori thanked the Border Reivers 'for their efforts in making available for me an Aston Martin and also a healthy youngster (Jim Clark) as co-driver to do most of the work for me. I must say that during those 24 hours I had very little confidence that this car would finish as its mis-firing was chronic – however, with all those Scotsmen in the pit just willing it to last, it obviously didn't dare give up the ghost completely . . . once again thank you to the Border Reivers and all those friendly Scotsmen associated with your effort.'

Later, when the Border Reivers came to sell the DBR1, it went to Roy Salvadori. In 1995, at the Coys Historic Meeting at Silverstone, Scott Watson had completely forgotten this fact, and in conversation with Salvadori remarked how cheaply they had sold the Aston – they had only got £1,000 for it and that included the old bus and the signalling equipment. Roy then chipped in and reminded Scott Watson that he and George Abecassis had jointly bought the car and the price was in fact only £900, and that it had taken them two years to find a buyer at £1,100. It was later reputedly sold to a Japanese for around £2 million. Scott Watson also recalled that according to his records the 1960 Le Mans was the only race in which the DBR1 ever finished, but the car did have some results in club racing in Scotland with Jim Clark.

The situation at Aston Martin in the early months of 1960 was best summed up by the late John Wyer in his book *That Certain Sound* (Edita SA, Lausanne). 'The DBR4, which might have won [Formula 1] races in 1958, was a dying duck in 1959 and stinking fish by 1960. At Monza in September 1959 our cars weighed 1,400 lbs, which was respectable by the standards of the Ferrari, the 250F1 Maserati and the Vanwall against which we would have been competing in 1958; at the same race the Cooper weighed 1,190 lbs and the new Lotus 1,080. John Cooper and Colin Chapman were busy driving nails into the coffin of the front-engined car.'

Seen with the brilliant clarity of today's hindsight, the entire programme defied logic. 1960 was to be the last year of the 2.5 litre Formula 1; it was to be replaced in 1961 with an engine capacity limit of just 1.5 litres, which was clearly going to play into the hands of the lighter cars, so Cooper and Lotus already had a head start. Moreover, Aston Martin were not going to produce an entirely new engine of this small capacity merely in order to continue to compete in Formula 1. It is therefore difficult to understand why the decision was not taken to close down the whole Aston Martin Formula 1 effort at the end of 1959 and perhaps concentrate more on a programme to develop a GT car to compete against Ferrari. But then if motor racing was ruled by logic it would be a very boring adventure for everyone concerned.

Even the lightweight version of the DBR4 was still not down to the fighting weight of the Cooper, and the new DBR5 still did not match up. As we have seen from Roy Salvadori's comments, the original DBR4 had a chance at the time when it was first tested, but as it progressed and evolved into the DBR5 things just went from bad to worse. Perhaps John Surtees was right not to sign for Aston Martin, as he was to compete with Lotus during the 1960 season when his motor cycle racing commitments allowed.

Meanwhile testing continued, but Jimmy Clark began to realise that his debut in Formula 1 might be delayed as all the effort was being concentrated on getting Roy Salvadori out racing the new car. When Reg agreed to let Jimmy out of his contract in order to drive a Lotus 18 at the 1960 Dutch Grand Prix and to allow John Surtees a drive, he little realised what was to happen. Clark joined Lotus, and the rest, as they say, is history.

Away from the day-to-day running of the team Reg got himself involved in other things concerning Aston Martin. Back in 1939 John Dugdale, writing in *Autocar*, posed the question as to which was Britain's fastest road car at that time, and it led to all sorts of controversy. This in turn led the Brooklands Automobile Racing Club to run a series of races at their Whitsun meeting that year, where private owners could bring their cars along and demonstrate what they could do. Since then there has been a continuous fascination about the maximum speeds of road cars, and some 20 years after the Brooklands event Reg had a small part in rekindling the controversy, and in turn helping Aston Martin to claim a new record. As already tried in 1958, the plan was to accelerate from 0 to 100 mph, then brake back to 0 again in the shortest possible time. In 1960 Aston introduced the DB4-GT and Reg did 0-100-0 in a remarkable 24 seconds. A year later, with the same model, he reduced this to 20 seconds, and this record stood for over three years until it was beaten by Ken Miles with a Shelby Cobra 427 with a time of 13.8 seconds!

Clearly Reg still loved driving and had not lost any of his skill. On an earlier occasion at Goodwood some young drivers were being given a test drive with the DBR1 under Reg's eagle eye. One of the drivers, taken round the circuit by Reg in an Aston Martin road car, got out of the car and said, 'By golly, the old bastard really knows his way round – that was quite an experience.'

At last, after the British Grand Prix, David Brown decided that to save any further humiliation and waste of time and manpower the entire racing programme should be stopped, so ten years of Aston Martin participation in motor racing came to an end. However, it was clear that a shrewd tactician like Reg would not stay unemployed in motor racing for very long.

What must be remembered is that even in 1960 the concept of commercial sponsorship outside the trade sponsors such as tyre manufacturers or oil and fuel manufacturers had not been pursued. However, during that year Ken Gregory, who ran BRP (British Racing Partnership), was approached by the three Samengo Turner brothers who ran the Yeoman Credit finance company, and as a result Yeoman Credit BRP raced that year in Formula 1 and opened up the possibility that companies outside motor racing might support the running of teams.

Towards the end of the 1960 season Yeoman Credit decided they wanted to break away from BRP, and the brothers approached Reg and offered him the chance to take over the running of their team. Needless to say he accepted on the spot, and so began his new career as team manager in Formula 1.

His first move was to get in touch with Gillian Harris. She had been offered the job of publicity manager at Aston Martin when Alan Dakers left, but she knew that Reg was about to join Yeoman Credit and had asked her to join him there, so she turned down John Wyer's offer at Aston Martin and moved to Yeoman Credit.

'I remember going for an interview at Yeoman House in Chiswick and being offered the job to work with Reg. We got premises out in Hounslow and some of the mechanics from Aston Martin came with us. This was a whole new aspect of racing for me, and after handling only 10 or 12 races a year I was thrown into something infinitely more complicated. Instead of moving 50 people to races like Le Mans, we were moving just a handful of mechanics and drivers, and the speed at which we had to work and turn round the cars became much more important.'

This was a completely new ball-game for Reg, and Roy Salvadori is quick to underline the situation: 'When Reg went to Yeoman Credit he had complete control of everything, and fortunately for him he took Gillian Harris with him, because he was the worst organiser. If he had to organise anything it was a complete disaster and it was Gill that held the team together. Without Gill the whole thing would have been a complete shambles. He wasn't allowed to do much fiddling about at Astons, as they were very strict about seeing that everyone had the same engines. A weakness with Reg was he would always play around. For instance, I remember at one time we were running Vandervell bearings and everyone was using Vandervell bearings but Reg went to Glacier for bearings and that didn't work. Much later there was the affair of the lightweight chassis when he put a Formula 1 engine into a Formula 3 chassis and that didn't work; Reg was into the bloody lot.'

Next there was the matter of drivers. Reg still had a hankering to have John Surtees with him, and he rang John towards the end of 1960 explaining his imminent move. Reg told him that they would be getting factory-prepared Coopers and would run as a parallel works team. Surtees explained that he was quite happy with Colin Chapman and Lotus, even though he admitted he was unhappy about the cars breaking. Reg told him he would kill himself if he stayed with Lotus, and Surtees admitted that 'it is true, I was worried, I was worried stiff, and I even became superstitious about it. I had Colin write in a clause in my contract to say that the team colours would be black for the 1961 season because I was starting to have a superstition about green. Remember it wasn't just one breakage we had – it was continuous. Colin was such a cavalier charmer, so talented, and his cars were so competitive. In fact, for me it was one of the few times a person could turn round and think that relative to the competition the most competitive cars you ever drove were in your very first year of racing. Basically the Lotus 18, when it hung together, was the best car, a super thing.'

However, behind the scenes Surtees had got himself embroiled in an internal team battle at Lotus. During the 1960 season the Lotus team had Surtees, Innes Ireland and Clark. Chapman asked Surtees who he would like to drive with in 1961. Being a straightforward and honest kind of person, he said he would like Jimmy Clark because he felt that he and Jimmy were closer in their attitudes to racing and they would not have the same friction that existed with Innes.

'At this all hell was let loose, as Innes got to hear about the conversation and kicked up a great fuss, so much so that Jo Bonnier and the Grand Prix Drivers Association got involved.'

Surtees was being blamed for it all and he told Chapman that he wanted to sit round a table with Innes and Colin and hammer it all out. In reply Colin explained that Innes had a contract, but that he was going to be team leader with BRP and they would run a parallel factory Lotus team. In turn Innes retorted, 'That's the first I've heard of it, and I'm not having it.' At this Surtees shrugged his shoulders and left it to Chapman and Ireland to sort things out.

So Surtees went back to Reg Parnell and was assured that Yeoman Credit would have the Cooper factory team with Roy Salvadori. There would be two teams running parallel, Cooper-Cooper and Yeoman-Cooper, producing a two-pronged attack.

Surtees: 'In fairness, knowing both John Cooper and Reg Parnell, I think they were both responsible because what happened of course was that we ended up with stock, bog-standard production cars, not the works cars.

'I think that John [Cooper] wanted to hold on to Reg and me as well and probably dreaming of some future. You have to remember that people like Reg and even myself, we are dreamers. Because of our enthusiasm, and Reg is one and I certainly know I am, we put together pictures thinking everybody else is just as enthusiastic as you are, then the practicalities come along. This is the difference between someone like me and, say, Jackie Stewart. He isn't a dreamer, he is just a plain, practical calculating person. I later dreamed of the creation of the Honda team, but you only have one career and you can waste a lot of time.'

So the Yeoman Credit team ended up with standard Coopers, but Reg still thought that everything would come out right because Harry Weslake had promised to work on the cylinder heads and give them more power, and other people had also made promises, but nothing really came of it.

As for his team mate, Surtees commented: 'I am also not sure that Roy Salvadori was happy with me around, as I was the new boy and I was very intense about everything. But Roy had a lot of experience and basically it was a good little team except that we were a totally private team competing against the works, and the only answer was to work on the cars ourselves. I suggested to Reg that we make some modifications to the Cooper, but it didn't really get us anywhere.'

During that season Salvadori, who was not so involved in the mechanical side of things, stood back and was clearly not impressed. 'We did better in the early part of 1961 with the standard Cooper, and I think that if Reg had left it to Coopers we would have been better off, for as soon as we started playing around with the car we began to have problems. Old Surtees loved to mess around with cars and was very interested in the mechanical side, but I'm not, so it didn't mean much to me, but the results we were getting were not working out. I think that under the rigid control of John Wyer or Lofty England we would have had more success and we needed someone to tell us what to do. I don't agree with drivers telling the team what to do, and that was what was happening.'

The 1961 grand prix season opened with Monaco, where only one Yeoman Credit Cooper was entered for John Surtees, who got as high as fifth place before the engine blew and he was out. A fifth place at Spa for Surtees was also a good placing, bearing in mind that this was a private team, and by the French Grand Prix Reg was able to field two cars, the second for Roy Salvadori, who finished eighth after John Surtees crashed. So it went on through the season, the best results being a second fifth place for Surtees at Nurburgring and a sixth for Salvadori at Monza.

Despite the rigours of running his own racing team, Reg decided to go to Le Mans. He got involved with his old friend Jock McBain of the Border Reivers, who were running their DBR1 there for the second time, this time with Ron Flockhart sharing the driving with Jim Clark. Meanwhile Gillian had been asked by John Webb (later of Brands Hatch fame, but at that time in the charter flying business) if she could help out as a stewardess for one of his charter flights for British race enthusiasts from Stansted to Tours, then by bus to Le Mans. This she did, and when at the race she too was roped in to help the Border Reivers. At the same event John Ogier's Essex Racing Team had entered an Aston Martin DB4 Zagato for Bib Stillwell and fellow Australian Lex Davison, and their pit was next to the Border Reivers pit. Sadly the car went out of the event reasonably early, and Stillwell wanted to get back to London quickly. He asked Gillian if there was a seat available on the charter flight and, as Gillian remarks, 'that was the beginning of this long and complicated life'. Some time later they were married and live today in Melbourne, Australia.

Chapter 13

1962-1964:
Reg Parnell Racing

BEFORE THE 1961 season had ended Reg Parnell and the Samengo Turners got down to discussing 1962, and what happened was influenced to a great extent by John Surtees. His opinion was that the only way in which to control more easily their destiny and have the best cars was to build them themselves.

'I felt that the only person likely to rival Colin Chapman was Eric Broadley at Lola. Lola and Lotus had run a parallel existence. I approached Eric, who lived just round the corner from where I lived in Bromley, and we reached an agreement whereby Yeoman Credit and Bowmaker [who had joined Yeoman] would supply the engines, etc., and Lola would supply the chassis for around £3,000 each.'

An official contract was drawn up, but the interesting point is that Eric Broadley wanted to deal with Surtees, so the contract was made with him, and he in turn had a contract with Yeoman Credit/Bowmaker to supply the cars to the team. One of the reasons for this was that Broadley wanted to ensure that Surtees was tied in as a team driver.

Meanwhile Ferrari had made an approach to Surtees and he had gone to Maranello to see them, but he felt that he did not have enough experience to join them; having worked with the Italians at MV Agusta he felt that he had to go into the team as a top level driver. He therefore shelved that option until a few years later.

The Lola deal was done, the cars were built, and they appeared for the first time at the fateful 1962 Goodwood Easter Monday meeting where Stirling Moss had the accident that finished his grand prix career. It had been very important to ensure that the team could get Climax V8 engines, so they arrived at the meeting with two brand new cars complete with the latest Climaxes.

Because of Moss's accident much of the detail of that race has been overlooked. The Bowmaker Lola was going very well first time out and Surtees and Moss, in the BRP Lotus, were taking turns in breaking the lap record after both had had pit stops. Initially, however, the car proved to be difficult to handle, particularly where there were changing road conditions. Even for Surtees, who was good in the wet, it was a problem, and the team couldn't get the car right.

Later, during practice at Spa when the car was jacked up to change wheels, Surtees noticed that the car had a twist. On the bumps of Spa the car had certainly not wanted to run in a straight line, so Eric Broadley immediately got down to the problem and added some extra tubes around the cockpit to stop the chassis flexing. As a result the car was totally transformed, and even came close to winning the German Grand Prix. However, being only a secondary team behind Climax's two favoured teams, Cooper and Lotus, and thus further down the queue, Reg had some difficulty getting their engines prepared. Indeed, it is amazing to note that the Bowmaker team were never able to do any serious testing of the cars between races due to the lack of engines, a situation unthinkable today when teams have rafts of engines available.

Reg, forever thinking up schemes, had the idea of approaching his friends at Maserati to get Maserati engines. Surtees recalls that 'Reg was a real wheeler-dealer. Above all he was a tremendous enthusiast. He was a straight-up guy except that he would perhaps pass on to you something that was less than actual fact by having his own vision clouded by his out-and-out enthusiasm. Sometimes in his enthusiasm he wouldn't listen to what the other person said, so he would go along and put his own interpretation on it. The end result was that it sometimes didn't work out that way, but it was not by intention. He was a competitor and, sure, there were certain people he didn't like, but on the other hand he was not a malicious person.

'Yes, he meddled a bit, and if I am honest I must admit that I am the same, but I think we both did these things for similar reasons. Reg did it because he felt he had to try and make up the gap between the equipment he had and the equipment other people had. He thought all the time that he had to try and reduce that gap and fight against it. Sometimes it worked and sometimes it was a negative feature and must have put the costs of the team up to a degree. If anything in that very early stage of my career in the racing world it could have possibly been better for me if Reg had been stronger. I think I learned a lot from Reg, and after that turbulent period at the end of 1960 when I had moved from one career to another and had all this turmoil take place, I felt I needed a period of stability and the fact that I stayed with Reg for two years showed the degree of faith I had in him. Some people would say he was a loveable rogue, but I can say from my experiences with him that he did what he said he would do, and if there was anything I would feel a bit unhappy about it was the situation at the very beginning and this business over the so-called works cars. That is something that has always left a little bit of a taste in my month, but he was someone who did an awful lot for the sport and I was only to learn much later that he was the man who was responsible for raising the standards of motor racing in Britain after the war.'

Towards the end of the 1962 racing season Coventry Climax told Reg that they would not be able to supply engines to his team for 1963, which caused Surtees to start and look for pastures new. BRM had approached him, but he shied away from that and instead took up the offer from Ferrari. He spoke to Reg about it, who agreed that in the circumstances it was probably the best move for him. However, Surtees is in no doubt about his loyalty to Reg Parnell: 'If Climax had offered us similar support to Cooper and Lotus then I probably would have stayed.'

During 1962 Reg had been approached by another motor cycling ace, Gary Hocking, who wanted to change from bikes to cars. Again Reg had been convinced that he had great potential, but had to explain that with John Surtees in the team it would put him in a difficult position. He also felt that there was no love lost between Surtees and Hocking, and the last thing he wanted was conflict in the team, so he was unable to help. However, later in the season, when Tim Parnell had an accident at Brands Hatch, it was arranged for Gary Hocking to drive Tim's Lotus at Mallory Park and Oulton Park, and he went extremely well. Reg promised to help, and in fact spoke to Rob Walker about Hocking, but tragically it was in one of Rob's cars that Hocking was killed in the South African Grand Prix the following year.

In preparation for the Tasman Series that winter Reg had a couple of the older four-cylinder 2.5 litre engines enlarged to 2.7, and with these the Lolas went like trains. They were tried out at Mallory Park and won, and went on to do so in Tasmania.

Before the end of the 1962 season Bowmaker decided to pull out of grand prix racing and offered the entire team to Reg at a very advantageous figure. While in Tasmania Reg noticed a young New Zealand driver called Chris Amon, and invited him to come over to Britain to take the place of John Surtees in his 1963 team, which was to be called Reg Parnell Racing.

At one of the early races in the season at Snetterton, Chris Ashmore arrived with his Ford Zodiac and double-decker trailer dragging a Formula Junior Lotus and a Formula 1 Cooper. The latter was a real starting money special for which Chris had paid the princely sum of £400.

'As I was pushing this ropy old Cooper to scrutineering Reg shouted over to me, "I don't know why you've come with that load of old rubbish wasting your time." I shouted back that I may be wasting my time but I'm on a bit of starting money thank you very much. Needless to say I qualified on the back of the grid. Halfway through the race I needed some water as the temperature was getting a bit high, so I pulled into Reg's pit because I had no pit staff of my own. I nipped out and pinched his watering can and topped up the radiator, and went back out on to the track only to see Surtees's Lola and later Amon's Lola parked at the side of the circuit, so I came in fifth. When I got back to the pits I pulled in beside Reg, got out and told him, "Well, Reg, it may be knackered but at least it finishes."'

The term 'shrewd' has often been used when describing Reg Parnell, and there is no doubt that this gruff-voiced Derby man, whose bark was much worse than his bite, kept his eyes open for new talent. He also kept watch on motor cycle racers, having already seen the talent in John Surtees. Now he noticed the son of an old pal of his from pre-war racing days, Stan Hailwood, who ran the huge motor cycle business Kings of Oxford. At that time Stan's son Mike was racking up the wins in international motor cycle racing for MV Agusta, but had a mild hankering after cars. Part of this was due to Reg, who felt he had a future in car racing, but Hailwood resisted.

Eventually Mike did try a racing car, but was not convinced. It was not until 1962 that he decided to switch from two wheels to four, and typically he went out and bought his own car, a Formula Junior Brabham, which he towed around the country. In his first race, at Brands Hatch, he finished second, and went on to win a few more events; ever confident, he decided that he needed to move up into something bigger. This coincided perfectly with another of Reg Parnell's bids to get him into one of his cars, so Mike Hailwood agreed.

Reg had left Bowmaker with the two V8-engined Lola-Climaxes and a Lotus 24 Climax V8, and although Hailwood had decided to continue to race for MV in 1963, more as a financial safety net, he would move into Formula 1 with Reg Parnell. Hailwood's relationship with Count Agusta was such that Agusta had thought about building a Formula 1 car. It is interesting to note that he actually paid

Hailwood a retainer of £2,500 a year as a carrot to lure him to drive it. In fact, the car was never built, so Hailwood had some extra pocket money for which he did not have to race.

As Reg was forming Reg Parnell Racing from scratch, Mike Hailwood agreed to take a half share in financing the team through his father Stan, so it was actually a Parnell/Hailwood team. Once again 'Uncle Reg' took a close personal interest in his new driver, and passed on a lot of valuable information to him. In Formula Junior the car was thrown about with little power to play with, but Formula 1 was different, as Hailwood was to find out on an initial test session at Silverstone with the Lotus Climax. Reg kept an eye on him lap after lap, and when he came in Reg seemed satisfied and commented, 'Considering the car and your inexperience you did well, but there's a lot of room for improvement. You've a lot to learn.'

As Hailwood had his own money sunk in the team he also made sure that he didn't wreck the equipment. At the same time, unlike Chris Amon who was paid as a professional racing driver, Hailwood got nothing save his expenses and some prize money. Although today a driver would bring sponsorship, Hailwood was paying for all of his racing as well as investing in the team out of his own pocket. But for him it was a valuable learning experience.

In 1962 the European motor racing scene saw the arrival of a young American called Peter Revson. Although he was a member of the Revlon cosmetic empire family, he was kept on a tight rein. He therefore had to gather together everything he had to buy a Formula Junior Cooper, which he dragged around Europe in a Thames van for a season's racing. As can be imagined, living out of a van was not much fun, but it was the normal way to go around Europe in those days. It must have been strange for an American who normally lived in some style, but it was clear that he was enjoying not only a freedom he did not have in America, but also a feeling of being closer to the action, where as a new driver he would have to shape up or ship out.

When he arrived in London he was looking for workshop space and met Reg in the Steering Wheel Club. Reg offered to help, so Revson moved into the Parnell premises.

He was successful in Juniors, and Reg was as always on the look-out for new talent, so he offered Revson a testing contract and a possible place in his Formula 1 team for 1963 alongside his two other fledgling stars, Chris Amon and Mike Hailwood. As it happened Revson only raced once for the team in 1963, at the International Gold Cup at Oulton Park, where he finished a creditable ninth. Later, after Reg's death, he bought Tim Parnell's Lola-bodied Lotus 24, running it as

Revson Racing (America) in 1964 but still alongside Reg Parnell Racing at Hounslow.

Around this time Reg had been in negotiation with the Australian Lex Davison, who had fitted the Lola chassis driven by John Surtees during the 1962 season with a 2.6 litre engine. The negotiations proved to be rather complicated due to the fact that although Bowmaker had pulled out, they were due to be paid some of the money. I am grateful to Diana, Lex's widow, for sending me some of the correspondence between Reg and Lex regarding these transactions, which amply illustrate Reg's penchant for wheeling and dealing, particularly when faced with a stubborn Australian.

At the time Reg was also acting as a kind of agent for Valerio Colotti, who manufactured gearboxes in Italy, and it was the gearboxes that were the bone of contention.

In March 1963 Lex was clearly having problems, and sent Reg the following telegram: 'New Colotti gearbox short many parts minor nature. May I recover from [Tony] Maggs Lola before shipment. Please cable authority. Cooper crown wheel and pinion required urgently for Palmer car. Regards Lex.'

In reply Reg cabled: 'Advise parts required Colotti gearbox and will forward better condition parts from UK or Italy. Despatching crown wheel/pinion Monday. Parnell.'

On 11 April Lex wrote to Reg saying, 'We are having frightful trouble with the Colotti gearboxes. The one attached to the [Masten] Gregory engine was on its last legs, with all gears badly pitted, and various pieces of selectors laying in the bottom of the box. I did manage two races with it (in both of which I defeated the Brabham of Stillwell and McKay) but the ZF did not appear to be working properly. Since the Victorian Trophy race we have had to make up one box from the two which I bought from you. The new box was incomplete and I think had been robbed of various parts during the Antipodean season. The crown wheel and pinion were not new but were not too badly marked for all that. There are no studs or nuts at all to hold the plates into the box, and generally, although the gears and the casing are new, it is very far from being a complete gearbox . . . I am coming to London in May. I would like to see you and have a drink at the Steering Wheel. Please do not dispose of all the Bowmaker Colotti parts before I get there, as I really am anxious to have a complete spare gearbox made up, and may even be interested in buying another complete "made up" box from you.'

A week later Lex again wrote to Reg: 'Bill Patterson had the misfortune to break a crown wheel and pinion in his Cooper box in practice, and I loaned him my spare box which had a straight cut crown wheel and pinion fitted. Phil Kerr had this made for me in England. It wouldn't appear to have been much good because it was brand new and Bill only managed three laps before he broke that one also.

'Could you procure three proper Cooper crown wheel and pinions for us and have them despatched as quickly as possible, two by air freight and one, which will be a spare, by ordinary surface mail.'

Things seemed to be calm for a month or two, then Reg wrote to Lex regarding the agreement: 'Sorry to trouble you again . . . but Bowmaker are extremely anxious to receive the £500 which is outstanding from the deal which we concluded during my stay in Australia. You will appreciate that it is now several months since the team was disbanded, and all these loose ends need to be tidied up as quickly as possible.'

Nothing much seems to have happened until early October when Lex wrote to Reg again about the Colotti gearboxes: 'I have had tremendous trouble getting together enough parts to be able to assemble a complete Colotti gearbox and at this date I still do not have a complete gearbox. . . In effect, I have had no spare gearbox for this year's racing. I am sure that both you and Bowmaker sold me the new type 32 gearbox as a complete entity, and you had no knowledge that the parts were missing, but I feel that it is only fair for you to put the case to Bowmaker for some reduction in the amount owing for all the expense and trouble incurred – a new type 32 box from Colotti would cost £550 sterling. By the time I have assembled the box bought from you it will owe me more than twice that much. I would be obliged if you would plead my case with Bowmakers to avoid me having to write to them on this matter.'

In reply Reg wrote: 'I was very disturbed that there should be further problems regarding the settlement of your account with Bowmaker: however, I approached them on the matter but they do not feel inclined to meet you on the cost of items bought for the Colotti box. You must admit, Lex, that you had ample opportunity to examine the equipment you were buying, and you bought the goods as they stood, seen and approved. It is really too late now to argue about the deal . . . I really do hope that this now finalises the whole deal . . .'

This was clearly a short fuse to Lex Davison, who replied: 'Arguments about gearboxes seem to have become an annual contest between us. Your statement that "it is really too late now to argue about the deal" and "that I had ample opportunity to examine the equipment I was buying, and bought the goods as they stood, seen and

approved" smacks very much of sharp used-car dealing. I have made
continuous complaints that the Colotti gearbox sold to me was not as
specified . . . in May we had a long conversation about all this. The
gearbox was sold to me as being brand new and complete, and I attach
a copy of our contract . . . Reg, it is really too bad that we must argue
over these matters. We decided that we must write everything down
so that there would be no arguments over who promised who what. I
will stand by the contract, but expect Bowmaker to do the same . . . I
am really surprised at the tone of your letter. I feel we have had a lousy
deal over this gearbox but quite realise that it was not your intention
to mislead me about its condition. Therefore, I cannot understand
why you argue the point when it seems so obvious that my claims are
justified . . .'

On 4 December 1963 Reg wrote his last letter on the subject: 'I do
contest your assertion that we are responsible for all the problems
which you have experienced with the Colotti gearboxes as this
appears to be the root of the trouble between us. I knew that the new
type 32 Colotti gearbox had some parts missing; immediately I
received your cable stating that "many parts of a minor nature were
missing" I asked you to let me have details of the parts so that I could
replace these. (Note that your cable said "minor nature" which could
not possibly include a crown wheel and pinion, and I would also point
out that a new gearbox is not supplied with ZF axle flanges.) With
regard to the other gearbox, I knew that this was a second-hand unit,
but I sold it to you in good faith believing it to be in racing condition.
And it must have been in racing condition, Lex, for in your letter of
April you mentioned that you had done two races with this gearbox,
beating Stillwell and McKay on both occasions, so despite the
problems you had experienced, it could not have been so very bad . . .
I strongly resent being accused of "sharp used-car dealing". . . . I really
find myself quite exhausted by it all and I am sure you are too.'

Lex's next letter was to Gillian, registering his shock and sadness at
Reg's death. Eventually a compromise was reached with Bowmaker
that cleared up everything – but not until November 1964!

During the 1963 season it was decided to buy one of the ex-Team
Lotus factory cars that Jim Clark had raced. Reg wanted to use the
BRM engine in it, but was advised against it by Colin Chapman when
Reg explained what he was going to do. As far as Chapman was
concerned the car had been designed for the Climax engine and not
the BRM, and in those days Chapman was careful to have everything
designed to only sufficient strength and reliability to suit the
components. For Hailwood, however, unversed in these things, Reg's

word and opinion was good enough, so the BRM engine was fitted. As it turned out the car was never quite right, not only the engine but also troubles with the new five-speed gearbox. Then there was the matter of handling, and Hailwood realised that perhaps Colin Chapman had been right after all.

The team finished the season with a few World Championship points, but that was all. Hailwood himself had only driven in two Grands Prix, his best finish being eighth in the British Grand Prix at Silverstone in the Lotus, followed by a tenth in the Italian GP at Monza. (Hailwood had also run in two non-Championship Formula 1 races for the team.)

Gillian Harris remembers that Reg was not feeling very well and had gone off to his room. 'He hadn't been well for some time and suffered badly from migraines. His recipe was a bottle of Worthington's and an aspirin, which usually did the trick, but I noticed that he got tired quite easily and would sleep a lot.'

Although Reg had carried over the Lotus and Lola cars from the previous season, Colin Chapman had introduced his monocoque Lotus 25 and made it clear that it was not going to be a customer car. The logical next move for Reg was therefore to build his own car. He was not alone in this, as Tony Robinson at BRP had already built one for that team.

For this new project Reg turned to Les Redmond, who had never seemed to get much credit for the Gemini Formula Junior cars he had built. At the time Redmond was working in North Wales on the various racing cars owned by Nick Cussons, of the soap-making family. At that time Sid Diggory was also involved in the garage, and they ran various Cooper Monaco sports cars and an Aston Martin DB4GT. Cussons, Redmond and Reg discussed the project and Redmond agreed to build the car, to be called the Parnell.

The chassis Redmond produced was the usual stressed-skin aluminium 'tub', but designed to accommodate all the other Lotus parts that Reg planned to use on the car. By late 1963 the car was well on its way, but by then Colin Chapman had decided after all to sell Reg two of his precious Lotus 25 chassis, so the Parnell project began to become somewhat superfluous. Nick Cussons recalls: 'We were well down the line and even had a dummy engine in it. The chief mechanic on the project was Derek Ongaro, and I must say the monocoque that Les Redmond produced was much stiffer than a Lotus.

'I remember that Les, Reg and I got together for lunch just a week before Reg died to decide what to do with the car, but then the tragedy struck and clearly Tim had enough on his hands taking up the team, so we just stopped work on the car.'

So the fledgling Parnell car, like the Challenger before it, was stillborn. One report claimed that the monocoque was destroyed, but Cussons said that in fact it was kept and eventually sold to someone in Scotland. Although I was close to the Scottish motor racing scene for many years, I never heard anything about the monocoque being in that part of the world, and certainly was not aware of any car built around it. Some of the parts, such as the suspension units and of course the engines, were retained and used by Reg Parnell Racing during the season on their Lotuses, while yet other parts eventually found their way into the Parnell-BRM sports car that Redmond also designed two years later, and which won nearly every race in which it competed with a new young driver called Mike Spence.

Recalling the Parnell Formula 1 car today, Tim is very honest about the decision: 'I was quite green at the time and finding my way, so we decided to stop the development of the new car and concentrate on the cars that existed. Then Colin came along and kept his word and delivered the two Lotus 25s, and this underlined that we had made the right decision.'

Some time after Christmas 1963 Reg Parnell was mucking about with a bulldozer back on the farm when he suddenly felt unwell and said that he was going home. When Tim arrived for his lunch he asked about his father and was told that he had gone to bed. When he didn't appear in the afternoon, Tim rang the doctor, who came and examined him. Reg had terrible pains in his stomach, and the doctor, thinking it was just wind, wrote a prescription and off he went. During the night Reg was in agony, and when the doctor came again he gave him something else to ease the pain and said that he would get him off to hospital after the holidays. Reg knew all the doctors in Derby as he had a great enthusiasm for holding cocktail parties for all his friends, including many doctors.

The next day he was still in great pain, so they took him into hospital and investigations showed that he had peritonitis. A drip was attached to his leg, but sadly this created a blood clot that went straight to his heart, and on 7 January 1964 Reg Parnell died at the age of just 53.

Tim remembers that sad day: 'All the doctors said it should never have happened, but there we are. It was terrible – at 53 he was still young and had handled everything in his life so well. My mother had died of leukaemia three years before. But I was grateful for the good education he had given me, which made me independent. Indeed, he used to get on to me about that, saying that sending me to boarding school was the worst thing he had done as it had made me so independent.

'At the funeral it amazed me to find out what a great man he was. I used to race in many countries and people would come up to me and tell me they were great friends of my father. At the opening race meeting at Anderstorp, Prince Bertil of Sweden told me how much he had enjoyed meeting my father.'

However, something else at the funeral stuck in Gillian Harris's mind. 'One of the saddest aspects of the funeral for me was that with all those people there and the pathway up to the door being banked with flowers, the vicar who gave the address never once referred to him by name, just "the departed", and I found that so unbelievable. Here was the funeral of this man of renown, and his name was never even mentioned.'

For Rob Walker it was a very tough blow. 'Many of my friends have died in and out of motor racing, but when Reg died I was ill for a week. He was a wonderful friend, and shortly before he died he said to me, "You know, Rob, you and I are the only two left of the real private entrants."'

To those who knew him Reg Parnell will be remembered as a tough competitor, a bluff, straight-talking man and also someone who never overlooked the main chance. He always chose the best drivers available and his preparation was meticulous. He was adept at creative inexactitude and, as Abraham Lincoln might have put it, he could fool some of the people some of the time. For example, it seems impossible that he could have bluffed a wily entrant like John Coombs who, when he finished his racing career, was a successful private entrant. It was at Silverstone and Reg had entered an Aston Martin, DB4GT for a Touring Car race in which Coombs had one of his beautifully prepared Jaguar 3.8 saloons entered for Roy Salvadori.

Coombs: 'So Mr Parnell got an entry with this bloody Aston Martin so I said, "Hold on, that car isn't homologated", to which Reg replied, "Of course it is". So I told him I hoped he would bring the necessary papers along with him the following morning at scrutineering when we can see whether it is homologated. Whereupon Reg arrived the next morning with a briefcase, came to where I was waiting with John Eason Gibson, the Secretary of the BRDC, and pulled out a brown envelope with "Aston Martin DB4" written on it, saying to John, "There are the homologation papers – would you disbelieve me?" John said that of course he would not disbelieve Reg, so they were allowed to run in the car and they won the race with it. Some two years later

Reg said to me, "You silly old booger, you didn't really think that car was homologated, did you?"'

Coombs recalls another occasion when Reg attempted to get Innes Ireland penalised during the 1962 Tourist Trophy race at Goodwood. Reg had entered John Surtees in a Maranello Concessionaires/ Bowmaker Ferrari 250GTO against a raft of other GTOs. In those days top drivers took part, and amongst the other competitors were Jim Clark in an evil-handling Aston Martin DB4GT Zagato, and Graham Hill in another Ferrari GTO entered by John Coombs. Ireland got a flying start in the UDT/Laystall Ferrari GTO but was being hounded by Surtees, Mike Parkes and Hill in the similar Ferraris and Clark in the Aston Martin. Later in the race Ireland came up amongst some back markers and, missing his braking at the chicane, took the escape road through the chicane and rejoined the track. Luckily for him the marshals said in their report that his avoidance was justified in the circumstances.

However, back at the pits this was not the view held by the team managers. As Coombs recalls, 'Reg came rushing down to me saying, "We've got to protest, we've got to protest!" Tommy Sopwith was running Mike Parkes in another Ferrari and he too got terribly excited and they were going to protest. I wouldn't join the protest because I felt it was not up to me, and if the organisers didn't penalise him, then it was up to them; Innes was also my great mate and I didn't want to have him penalised. So off they stomped, but by that time John Surtees had been put out when he hit Jim Clark's Aston Martin, which had finally decided to slide off the road, so that was that. I shouted to Reg and asked him why he wasn't going to protest any more, and got a few gruff remarks from him. Innes won the race by just 3.4 seconds ahead of my Ferrari driven by Graham Hill. Had Innes not taken the short cut we certainly would have won that race, but Reg was all for having him disqualified.'

To Henry Taylor, who competed in his first grand prix in Tim Parnell's Cooper, Reg was 'a typical Derbyshire farmer and a very nice man too. There was nothing wicked or crooked about Reg. He was firm but was such a good team manager to us youngsters at the time in a manner in which I feel modern managers do not know how to be. They are all tuned into money and computers – it's a different world today.

'I remember in 1960 I drove a Ferrari 250GT with Graham Whitehead at Le Mans. It was wet and Graham had obviously frightened himself and came into the pits completely unexpectedly after only about ten laps. We had agreed to do two-hour stints and I had already completed two hours, but I remember Reg coming to the caravan where I was resting and in his typical, very gruff Sergeant Major voice shouting, "Get back in that f---ing car and go!" So I took over and at the end of the next two hours I came back to the pits and got out, but again Reg shouted, "Get back in that bloody car again", and to be honest I didn't really know at that time what was going on, but realised that he was the Sergeant Major and you didn't ask why, you just got in and you drove. Clearly Graham was in such a state that he would not be able to drive again for a few hours. But that was Reg Parnell – even though he was not directly involved with Le Mans that year, he was in the pit helping out his friends the Whiteheads.'

Perhaps some time Reg Parnell will receive the recognition he deserves. He worked hard at motor racing and came from the 'wrong side of the tracks' to become one of the best racing drivers in the world. He was brilliant in the wet and always said that driving in rain was easy. He used to tell anyone who would listen that provided you always braked in a straight line and took the inside line on the corners, you could brake much later than you thought, and he proved this on many occasions.

Had the war not intervened he might have reached the very top with a full factory drive with one of the Italian teams, but who is to say? His bluff manner made him appear fearsome, but as we have seen he had a sharp sense of humour and never suffered fools. Strangely enough, he always looked older than he was, and it may have acted against him, although this could be discounted when one considers the number of pre-war racing drivers who were running in grand prix teams at the time. We have seen that he was a 'meddler', and that might have ruled against him, but John Surtees was also so inclined and he became World Champion.

Perhaps history will finally judge Reg Parnell as one of the world's great drivers who was disadvantaged by the fact that he was British when it was Italian teams that dominated the scene and when British motor racing at grand prix level was in poor shape. Motor racing was rather more nationalistic in those days, and Reg's great relationship with Maserati might have seen him in one of their cars. But Maserati in the 1950s used motor racing as a commercial weapon, and favoured the Argentines as they were seeking lucrative machine tool contracts in South America at the time.

Without Reg Parnell and his partner Joe Ashmore we might not have seen any half decent cars racing immediately after the war. He and Joe took a risk on the war ending in victory for the Allies, and like many others made some very shrewd investments in old racing cars.

Happily many people have made some equally shrewd investments in old racing cars in recent years, which is why, although Reg may not be with us any more, we can still see and hear those classic cars of the past like the Maserati 4CL and 4CLT, and the ERAs that helped Reg on his way.

Reg Parnell will always be remembered by many people as the epitome of true British grit in the face of overwhelming odds, the stuff of which heros are made. And to many Reg Parnell was a hero.

Epilogue

Tim Parnell and Parnell Racing

REGINALD HAROLD HASLEM (Tim) Parnell was born on 25 June 1932. His mother was Gladys, who was Reg's first wife. She died in 1960 and Reg married his second wife, Betty, in 1962.

Tim's middle names, Harold Haslem, came from within the family. Harold Haslem, the son of Reg's cousin, was a choirboy and was killed when cycling to St Paul's church in Derby. The front wheel of his bicycle was caught in a tram rail and he was thrown in front of a steam roller. Haslem was Gladys's family name, and of course Reginald came from his father.

'My father thought my name was shocking, in fact I don't think he was even present at my christening because he couldn't believe they had given me all those names – so he always used to call me Tim!'

Even when he was small his father sometimes took him to the races.

'I remember going down to London as a little lad, and when we got to the gates of Brooklands my father said to me, "Look, you'll have to get under this blanket because I have no tickets to get you in", so they hid me under this blanket to get into the circuit . . . another time he took me to Donington because there was a Soap Box Derby where the Boy Scouts were pedalling round the circuit, and on that occasion I remember seeing Prince Bira win a race. As a Siamese Prince he was coloured, and of course being a little lad it interested me to see this person of a different colour . . . those are the sort of things you remember.'

During the early part of the war Tim had a normal childhood on the farm, although he and his friends had barns full of racing cars to play with.

'During the war all the kids used to come to our farm and we used to sit in the cockpits of these racing cars and have a wonderful time. Father would come home and go absolutely bananas.'

One of the cars was the Alfa Romeo 8C, which had been raced by Hans Reusch and Dick Seaman and had been bought by Robert Arbuthnot, a Scot who lived in England. This was Tim's favourite, and when the kids came round he always took the Alfa, whereas the rest had to make do with the odd ERA or Riley.

He remembers being taken by his father to visit Arbuthnot in what he thought was a castle with walls feet thick. 'Arburthnot told me that when he was a boy he used to ride his bike round on top of the walls of this castle, and of course I looked at him in amazement. As far as I recollect he more or less asked my father to take the Alfa away when the war started as the army had requisitioned the castle and if he left the car there would be nothing left after the war. But this went on all the time.

'As my father was delivering shells and food around the country as part of essential war work, there was many a night when the lorries would come back to Derby all sheeted up with racing cars under the sheets.'

One of the things that Reg gave Tim, which he had not had himself, was a good education. Tim was sent to Oakham School in Rutland as a boarder until he was 18. His father wanted him to be a farmer and take over the running of the farm, so when he left school he was sent up to Scotland to Chalmers Watson's famous dairy farm, Fenton Barns, near North Berwick to the west of Edinburgh. He stayed there for a year and got to know that part of Scotland well.

Reg was as successful and innovative in farming as he was in motor racing. He raised pigs and cattle; originally they had Ayrshires, but then moved into Friesians. Tim still has the farm, the land and the cattle, but the pig farm was closed down and the big family home, Wallfield House, is now a nursing home.

Reg was one of the pioneers of the Landrace pig, which originated in Sweden. It was a very long animal and had two extra ribs, which made it ideal for bacon and ham. Stirling Moss's father, Alfred, raised Large Whites, then went into rabbit farming with a strain imported from New Zealand. As they knew each other very well, Alfred got Reg interested in rabbits and he started to raise them both for meat and their pelts. One tends to forget that in many areas of Britain in the 1950s rabbits were commonplace on butchers' shelves, and it was only the myxomatosis epidemic of the late 1950s that both wiped out a large section of the rabbit population and turned people against eating the meat.

However, after school and his apprenticeship Tim wanted to go motor racing. 'I could see why my father never wanted me to be involved in motor racing. It was very dangerous in those days, there was no doubt about it. In the '50s half of the starting grid for a race would be wiped out within three or four years.

'He was also very hard with money and never used to give me much, which I now think was wonderful. He really taught me the value of money and it was one of the best lessons he could possibly have given me. But you must remember that he was a terrific wheeler-dealer, whether it was cars or pigs. He always used to say to me, "If we're taking profit we'll never go broke . . . don't kill the goose that's laying the golden egg." As long as he was taking profit on something he would sell it.'

Eventually, by fair means and foul, Tim scraped together enough money to buy a Le Mans Replica Frazer Nash, which he saw advertised by another former racing driver, John Young. He hardly raced this car and in its place bought one of the early Bobtail Cooper sports cars on hire purchase.

At that time starting money in Britain was anything between £75 and £100, and nearer £250 abroad, so by spending upwards of six weeks on the continent wandering from Sweden to Italy and Austria sometimes a profit could be made.

Once Tim had competed in a few events and done reasonably well his father began to help him. His first season with the Cooper sports car was one of the most enjoyable, as this 1,100 cc Climax-powered class provided tremendous racing. Many of the British stars of those days emerged from that class, where Cooper, Lotus, Elva, Lola and even Arthur Mallock with his U2 were all battling it out on the circuits.

Tim then bought a Formula Junior Cooper into which he put one of Keith Duckworth's early Cosworth engines. Tim had met Duckworth when he first started up business in a lock-up garage in a pub yard: 'I got a Cosworth off him to put in the Cooper, but the Cooper-Cosworth couldn't stay with a Lotus 18 when it came to road-holding. I remember an incident with Keith that happened at the famous Steering Wheel Club in London when I arrived without my membership card. I insisted I was a member but I think they thought I was a plain clothes policeman out to check on the licensing laws. Luckily Keith saw the problem I was having and explained who I was and I was allowed in. It is a great pity we don't have a private club for racing drivers like that nowadays. On a Thursday night Cliff Davis, Steve Ouvaroff, Peter Jopp and Les Leston, all great racing worthies in their day, used to prop up the bar – fortunately there were few drink-and-driving crusades and no breathalysers! Mind you, I don't know if racing drivers go out for a drink these days.

'When I saw how good the Lotus 18 was I went to see Colin Chapman and told him that I would like one as they looked pretty good to me. Typically, Colin noticed a brand new one ready to be sent the next day to the USA and said, "Seeing it's you, you can have that one." To this day I don't know when that poor American guy ever got his Lotus 18.

'I remember one year at Reims with Trevor Taylor, Mike McKee and me in Formula Junior Lotus 18s qualifying for the FJ race, which ran as an opener to the French Grand Prix. There were 100 bottles of champagne for the person setting up fastest lap in practice, and we were struggling. Trev and I were slipstreaming each other and discovered that if you went down the slip road at Thillois, turned the car round and came barrelling out again you got an extra 300 revs by the time you reached the start and finish line. This meant you were quicker into your next lap. Trevor got the fastest lap by slipstreaming me and so won the 100 bottles.

'Trev made a bad start in the first heat and in the final Mike McKee and I led between us until on the last lap Mike beat me by a fifth of a second.

'Back in those days we used to have fantastic prize-givings and at Reims we went back to the town hall and there was no doubt about it, the French Grand Prix was a real social occasion.

'After the town hall affair we all used to adjourn to Bridget's Bar where all sorts of things would go on and people used to get thrown into the pond in the garden. On this occasion when we arrived the place was solid, you could hardly move or reach out for your drink. Bridget was panicking because there were far too many people in the pub, so she rang for the gendarmes to try and control the situation. When they arrived they started ordering people about and nobody was taking a blind bit of notice. I was standing beside Trevor Taylor and his brother Mike, who was his mechanic, when suddenly the police had had enough of this and started shooting their guns in the air. We ran off as it was getting serious, and people were diving under cars.

'The next thing I knew a policeman grabbed hold of me and put a sub-machine gun in my stomach – of course I didn't offer too much resistance. One of Trevor's friends was arrested with me and we were put in a black maria to take us to the police station. Of course this was all outside Bridget's where you had this great congregation of mechanics and drivers. Our black maria set off at high speed and there was an enormous crashing sound as the entire rear bumper was torn off because some wag had tied it on to a tree! 'There was more uproar, the doors of the van were thrown open and more bodies were thrown in. We set off again and there was a hell of a lurch and we all fell on top of each other because someone had undone the wheel nuts on the front wheel and the front wheel fell off. Now there was absolute chaos. The gendarmes were furious, two more black marias arrived and we were taken down and put in jail. Most of the people arrested just had their names taken and were let free, but Trevor Taylor's pal and I, for some reason or other – I think because I had threatened one of the policemen with violence with the way he was going on – were put into a proper cell. The next thing I knew people were banging on the windows and the doors of the jail, and apparently Stan Elsworth, my father's mechanic from the old days, had got all the people together and they marched on the jail and were banging on the doors and windows to get the gendarmes to release us. So the gendarmes took us to the back door of the jail and let us go, then went back to the front and took two of the representatives including Stan into the jail to show them that we were not in jail. What an evening that was.

'When we went back to England after the race at Reims Trevor Taylor and I called in at Keith Duckworth's little workshop at the pub and took all his lads into the greasy spoon caff at the corner for a slap-up, and we put some of the bottles of champagne on the table, which the lads drank out of plastic cups. Keith often remembers that.'

Tim moved up into Formula II with a Cooper built by himself at the Cooper factory in the time-honoured way.

'Charlie Cooper – John Cooper's father – was a cantankerous bugger and used to wander round saying to no one in particular, "What do these people know about motor racing – what's he doing?" It was an education to work at Coopers.

'I remember when building my Formula II car the bits van would arrive from suppliers and you had to put them all on your car right away and guard your car until it was finished, then whip it out of the factory. There was one Australian who had got his car almost finished and he went on holiday for a week. When he came back half the bloody car had been nicked to finish other people's cars. These were hilarious and wonderful days at Cooper, and there would be around ten cars being built, but you had to have your own mechanics there to see you got your car finished.

'My worst racing experience was at Aix le Bains when a spectator bridge collapsed during the race and poor old Chris Threlfall was killed as he drove under it. I've never seen anything like it – it was like a battlefield. Then later on in the 1961 Italian GP at Monza, Wolfgang Von Trips in his Ferrari and Jimmy Clark in his Lotus came together and Von Trips's car went into the crowd and an awful lot of people were killed. The race continued and I couldn't believe it when they started to lay all the bodies along the side of the race track while we were racing, which I thought was horrendous.'

At one time Tim formed a loose team with his pal Gerry Ashmore – son of Joe – and the Belgian driver André Pilette, which they called the Three Musketeers. At the time the leading Belgian racing driver was Willy Mairesse who used to get involved in the most incredible accidents with various Ferraris. Recalling those days Tim remarks, 'I remember André Pilette telling me that "Willy Mairesse is absolutely crackers". . . Mairesse used to ride horses and would ride them straight through hedges and fences and create all sorts of mayhem with them.'

Had Tim not been around, the tragic and sudden death of his father could have put a stop to everything. Although he had been racing privately in Formula 1 with his own car as R. H. H. Parnell Ltd, Tim had also been involved with his father's team and had been brought up on motor racing.

Roy Salvadori recalls the early days at Aston Martin when Tim was a growing, but hefty, lad: 'He was always at Le Mans and was a good worker; Reg got good value out of him and as he was a big boy he was handy in case we needed a "chucker-out" in the pits.'

Tim had many friends in motor racing and they rallied round him in those fraught early days of 1964 when he was faced with having to take over the helm for a Formula 1 season.

'The people who were sponsoring my father's team in 1964, the fuel and tyre companies, told me that if I wanted to take over they would give me their full support.

'Colin Chapman had arranged to let my father have the use of two Lotus 25 monocoque cars, and Wally Hassan of Coventry Climax promised my father the experimental which he had run in 1963 for Chris Amon. It was a marvellous set-up and I had their backing, but they made it clear to me that they did not think I should drive but should concentrate on doing this job.

'I gave up my driving and Peter Revson took over my Lotus 24 BRM, which I had last raced in the 1962 Austrian Grand Prix, and ran it alongside our team of Chris Amon and Mike Hailwood.

'Peter, Chris and Mike lived in Ditton Road, in Surbiton,

Surrey, and absolutely terrified all the neighbours and the local police, but that's another story. They called themselves the Ditton Road Gang and I think they had wild parties every weekend they were not racing.

'As for giving up my own racing, I felt I had to give our team a go for a year to see what happened, and as it went quite well we carried on.

'Another person who was always helpful to me was Colin Chapman. I remember once when Mike Hailwood put our Lotus 25 into the lake at Enna, Colin immediately lent me another car for the Austrian Grand Prix complete with a Climax engine. No matter what others say, Colin was a great lad as far as I was concerned.

'The best stroke of luck I had in those early days came from Sir Alfred Owen and Tony Rudd at BRM. They loaned V8 BRM engines to my father and he used them in his Lotus 24 in 1963. They also let me have one for my own Lotus 24, but my father being my father saw to it that I ended up with a Lola body on my Lotus, and it was in that state when Peter Revson drove it. In fact, even today people ask me why the Revson car had a Lola body, and that was my father – he was always tinkering about and swopping bits, as with the Delages and the ERAs he owned.

'Tony Rudd is a great friend of mine and I have always been grateful for what he did for me in motor racing. They said to me after I took over the team that if I was prepared to run their reserve driver, Dickie Attwood, in our car they would supply me with BRM engines and help run it, which was a terrific asset in those days. We fitted them to our Lotus 25 monocoque chassis (numbers R3 and R7) for the 1964 season.'

At the end of the 1964 season Mike Hailwood withdrew his support from the team and Tim Parnell took over the entire running and financing. He was given great support in this by people like Dennis Druit of BP, Keith Ballisat of Shell and Laurie Hands of Champion plugs.

During the 1966 season Hollywood invaded the grand prix world for John Frankenheimer's film *Grand Prix*, which starred James Garner, Yves Montand and Eva Marie Saint, and some dummy racing cars had to be built for the film. One day French journalist Bernard Cahier, who was acting as a consultant to Frankenheimer, asked whether Tim would be interested in supplying some cars. 'I told him that if there was any money in it I was interested. Chris Amon was involved in some of the driving and I was left with the feeling that making films seemed to be such a boring life, the way you stand about for days. I was very impressed with John Frankenheimer, however, and how he put that film together.'

A strange thing happened at the 1966 Italian Grand Prix, which once again reflected the reputation that Reg Parnell had around the world. Tim had entered Mike Spence and the young Italian driver Giancarlo Baghetti for the race, driving Lotus 33s with BRM engines. The Automobile Club in Milan had written to Tim to ask specifically if he would provide a car for Baghetti, and in return they would give an excellent financial inducement, so the deal was done.

Tim was using Lotus 33s with 2 litre BRM engines as they did not yet have a 3 litre engine, even though it was nearly the end of the first season of the 3 litre formula. Their pit was next to the Ferrari pit, and during practice Eugenio Dragoni, the Ferrari team manager, brought Enzo Ferrari over to meet Tim.

'I had met Enzo Ferrari before with my father, and they could see that Baghetti was doing quite well in our underpowered car. Mr Ferrari then told me he had with them their little Ferrari, the 2.4 litre interim car (chassis 158/0006), and would we like it for Baghetti?

'We said Christ, yes, of course we would, and he gave us the car. It was wheeled into our pit along with a couple of Ferrari mechanics.'

In the race Baghetti had trouble and called into the pits, and although he finished the race he was unclassified and Mike Spence finished fifth.

At the final grand prix of the 1966 season in Mexico, Tim, who had been running Innes Ireland alongside Richard Attwood, finally lost patience with Innes's occasionally cavalier attitude towards racing. He explains:

'We got to the race track early in the morning with practice due to start about three in the afternoon, but there was no Innes – he just didn't turn up. Bob Bondurant was hanging around the pits and I said to him that he had better drive the car. Bondurant had driven for me in a Formula 2 car in France when David Hobbs had had an accident on the way to the circuit, and was down in Mexico just to watch the race.

'With half an hour to go before the end of practice Innes arrived all laughing and joking and telling me he had got lost in the traffic. I told him it was bloody half past four in the afternoon and how the f--- can you get lost at half past four in the afternoon!

'Innes got all stroppy and I told him that if that was how he felt I would just leave Bob Bondurant in the car, and as far as I was concerned he had had it. Of course the story went down the pits like bloody wildfire. All sorts of people came up to me and said, "Well done, that was a damned good move of yours." But I was determined to make these drivers take notice and arrive on time. Of course we made it all up and Innes drove for me in the next grand prix, which was the South African.'

At the end of the 1966 season Tim received a telephone call from Tony Rudd, who was at that time up to his eyes in the development of the BRM H16 engine, to say that BRM wanted to do the Tasman Series. He explained that he couldn't possibly go out there or devote many of his mechanics to the Series, so if he gave Tim two BRM V8s and two mechanics, would he go and do the Series for them with Jackie Stewart and Graham Hill as the drivers?

'I took one of my own mechanics, Stan Collier, with me, and as we now all know we had a hell of a success. The Tasman was a wonderful Series, and for me it was like going back to the type of motor racing we had before the war as I remembered it.'

However, when they arrived in Australia it became necessary to alter the configuration of Stewart's car and install one of the H16 engines with the exhaust in the centre rather than at the sides, and Hill was not pleased about that.

'When you were working with Graham Hill you had to do everything 100 per cent. It was very serious stuff – there was no larking about. When you were dealing with him you always had to give him positive answers. Once practice was over, there was a marvellous change in his personality. He appreciated the mechanics, bought them beers and treated them well, but he was really tough to work with.'

Quite a few problems had to be sorted out, but as Tim was quick to point out, 'Graham and Jackie were so determined to win, they were real winners. They never drove under strict orders from me. They knew what they had to do and what was expected of them, and the last thing I wanted to happen was for them both to knock each other off the road. I told them that if they did that, there would be hell to pay. The main opposition was Jim Clark, Jack Brabham, Denny Hulme and of course Chris Amon with the Ferrari – it was almost like a blinking Formula 1 grid out there, yet Graham and Jackie went out and did the business and we won the Championship.'

This turned out to be a successful adjunct to Reg Parnell Racing and Tim was to run the BRM teams at the subsequent Tasman Series in 1967 and 1968.

Another of Tim's little side tasks was to work with Jochen Rindt on a series of racing car shows around Europe. Tim would make the arrangements with the teams to borrow cars and would transport them to these shows in Germany and Austria.

'I always remember going to Frank Williams' workshop to arrange for one of his cars to go, and arrived when they had just had all the office furniture repossessed. Of course Frank's vital lifeline was the telephone – he use to work as a night watchman in a service station, but that didn't last long once the telephone bills started to come in.

'Anyway, I offered Frank £75 for the loan of his car for this show. He looked around and asked if I could make it £100 as things were very tight. So I told him I would give him the money provided he didn't tell anyone else I had given him more.

'I remember one of these shows held in Hungary where we couldn't get anything sorted out because you couldn't change Hungarian money. Then Jochen had an idea and contacted the Austrian version of the RAC, and it was arranged that we would be paid in Hungarian petrol coupons, which the Austrian RAC converted into money for us – presumably they would then sell the Hungarian coupons to members wanting to visit Hungary who could take petrol coupons with them.

'I always got on well with Jochen, great lad, and I always seemed to get on with Austrians like Niki Lauda and Helmut Marko. Helmut was a hell of a good racing driver until he had that terrible accident at Clermont Ferrand when a stone was thrown up from Ronnie Petersen's car and it went right through his visor and into his eye. He could get a car at the most amazing angles and still catch it and hold it.

'Niki Lauda was absolutely dedicated to motor racing. If we went for a day's testing [with BRM] he was always frightened to get out of the car in case I put anybody else in it. There was no doubt about it, at that time he was going to make it to the top. Like most of today's drivers you have to be a bit mean and selfish to get on.

'It was a great tragedy for BRM when we lost both Jo Siffert and Pedro Rodriguez in the same year. Jo in particular had done a lot of the work to get Marlboro interested in motor racing, and of course he was doing very well with us. We then became associated with the French Motul company, which is why we got involved with Jean Pierre Beltoise, Henri Pescarolo and Francois Migault, but it was a hell of a struggle from then on.

'We should never have lost that Marlboro contract, and I feel that Louis Stanley didn't handle the Marlboro situation very well. Mind you, the aggressiveness of some of the Marlboro people in some of the countries we went to was quite amazing.'

By the end of 1968 Reg Parnell Racing was struggling, and over at BRM there was a massive upheaval following the demise of the H16 project. Tony Rudd, who was a key figure in the team, left to join Lotus, and Sir Alfred Owen called Tim for a meeting.

'He asked me if I would come and look after the team, and at the same time would I like to become Works Manager to ensure that the works operated to full capacity? I was very fortunate at the time because Tony Southgate, who was working with Dan Gurney's Eagle team, was looking out for a position back in England in Formula 1.

'I immediately put him in touch with BRM, they took him on and so I was there with Tony Southgate when we started, and he designed the fabulous 153, 160 and 180 BRMs, which were all very successful cars.'

To Tim Sir Alfred Owen was someone special:

'He was one of the most remarkable men I have ever met. He was the chairman of over a hundred companies at the time, was on the Government Savings Committee council, one of the Government transport committees, was Chairman of Dr Barnardo's Homes and was also a Methodist lay preacher.

'There were many times when he wanted to see me or I wanted to see him, and his secretary, Miss Ramsden, with whom I got on very well, would work wonders and fit me in between him going from one meeting to another. He would be at a meeting in London and I had to be waiting outside the meeting where we would jump into a taxi and while we were driving across London to his next appointment we would discuss various things, then he would jump out of the taxi saying, "Well done, Tim, carry on . . . and, oh, pay the taxi and put it on the expenses", and then he would be off into another meeting.'

Late in 1968 Sir Alfred Owen had a heart attack, and his sister and brother-in-law Jean and Louis Stanley took over the running of the BRM team. Tim continued as team manager and was able to engage a number of good drivers; he had a particular liking for Pedro Rodriguez, the young Mexican driver. 'I had seen him around for a long time and as a sports car driver he was the tops without a doubt. I think in all fairness that his younger brother Ricardo was better. I remember when they first came to Le Mans as teenagers driving for Luigi Chinetti, they were as fast in the dark as they were in the daylight.

'Pedro was the godfather to my son Michael and it was a great tragedy that he was killed like that. [He was offered a drive in Herbert Muller's Ferrari 512M sports car for the Norisring. In the race he had a huge accident where the car burst into flames, having, I believe, suffered a puncture.] I implored him not to go to that race at the Norisring. The team [BRM] was really going well and we were right up there. These people at the Norisring kept ringing him and offering him more and more money. I think it really was a clapped-out car. Of course, knowing Pedro he was up there in front in this car because that was all he knew, to win or to lead, and I believe he went off at a place where the Armco had been removed and the ambulance was standing. It was a great loss.'

At the beginning of 1975 Tim left the BRM team because Rubery Owen were going through a bad patch and David Owen, Sir Alfred's son, was cutting back on all their involvements. He and his brother John decided that they would stop racing, and when Tim left the team was taken over by the Stanleys and renamed Stanley-BRM.

Tim returned to the farm, content to continue his life away from motor racing. However, a chance telephone call from John Webb of Grovewood Securities, who owned a number of British circuits, offered him the chance to oversee both Mallory Park and Oulton Park as Regional Director. He took that position for a few years, but left when Mallory Park was sold to Chris Meek. Looking back on it now he feels he should have put in an offer and bought the circuit himself, but he was too late in thinking about it.

However, that was not the end of his involvement with circuits, as Tom Wheatcroft found himself with a number of problems at Donington Park and his Managing Director, Robert Fearnell, approached Tim to come and help out. It was at the time when Wheatcroft was in the midst of the negotiations for both car and motor cycle grand prix races, and the 'war' was at its height.

'I've never walked into a position where there were so many writs on the table,' says Tim. 'It was unbelievably complicated and I advised Tom that we had to find a compromise. I have worked with some tough characters like Louis Stanley and John Webb, but this was unbelievable. Finally we managed to get the circuit homologated for Formula 1.

'Tom is a remarkable man in what he has done for motor racing. He has built up an empire, but I think that being a builder he just likes to take on authorities and loves getting legal people involved in things.'

Like his father, Tim was good at spotting new talent, and I asked him which driver was the best he had worked with. Without hesitation he picked Niki Lauda, but qualified his remark: 'I think, however, the most unlucky and talented guy was Chris Amon. The natural ability he had was phenomenal. The nicest guy and one I enjoyed working with was Mike Spence. He was a wonderful chap on testing . . . then Colin borrowed him from us to run at Indianapolis and he was killed testing the gas turbine Lotus just a few weeks after Jimmy Clark had been killed.'

All of this is long behind Tim Parnell now. Today he is a very active member of the Board of the British Racing Drivers Club, keeps his farm running near Derby and is one of the most cheerful and friendly faces you could meet at a race. Like his father, he has contributed and is still contributing his own skills to motor racing, but neither of his two sons seems likely to take up a motor racing career like their father or their illustrious grandfather Reg Parnell.

Appendix

Race Results, 1935-1963

THE FOLLOWING IS an incomplete set of race results for both Reg and Tim Parnell. I am indebted to the tremendous work done by Paul Sheldon and Duncan Rabagliati in their monumental work *A Record of Grand Prix and Voiturette Racing*, Volumes 1-6. They did nearly all the work detailed below and their books are amongst the most informative available. However, as they only cover single-seater racing cars I have sought to add other races in which the Parnells competed, but regrettably I am sure it remains far from complete.

Reg Parnell's races

Date	Event	Circuit	Car/Chassis	Result
1935				
2 July	Nuffield Trophy	Donington	MG K3 Magnette	Ret'd: big-end
17 Aug	10-lap Handicap	Donington	MG K3 Magnette	1st
1936				
4 April	British Empire Trophy	Donington	MG K3 Magnette	No information
9 May	5-lap Handicap	Donington	MG K3 Magnette	5th
	10-lap Handicap	Donington	MG K3 Magnette	3rd
3 July	Nuffield Trophy	Donington	MG K3 Magnette	Ret'd: crash/ brakes locked
15 Aug	Locke-King Trophy	Brooklands	MG K3 Magnette	Ret'd: engine trouble
29 Aug	Junior Car Club 200	Donington	MG K3 Magnette	Flagged off, 71 laps
19 Sept	BRDC 500	Brooklands	MG K3 Magnette	Ret'd lap 4: broken piston

1937

24 Apr	Coronation Trophy	Crystal Palace	MG K3 Magnette	No finish
3 June	RAC Light Car Race	Douglas IOM	MG K3 Magnette	12th
17 July	Campbell Circuit	Brooklands	MG K3 Magnette	No information
20 Aug	Junior Car Club 200	Donington	MG K3 Magnette	Unclassified 8th; 5th in small class
	Brooklands 500	Brooklands	MG K3 Magnette	Accident in practice with Kay Petre

Competition licence taken away by RAC

1938

Reg Parnell did not race during this season due to his RAC ban. However, he continued to enter his Magnette for races with other drivers. In December 1938 his licence was reinstated for the 1939 racing season.

1939

11 Mar	2nd March Handicap	Brooklands	BHW	3rd
	3rd March Handicap	Brooklands	BHW	2nd
25 Mar	2nd Mountain Handicap	Brooklands	BHW	2nd
? May	Mountain Handicap	Brooklands	BHW	3rd
10 June	Nuffield Trophy	Donington	Challenger	Did not arrive – car not finished

1946

22 Apr	Elstree Speed Trials	Elstree	Maserati 4CL	3rd
19 May	Prescott Hill Climb	Prescott	Maserati 4CL	Not known
15 June	Gransden Trophy	Gransden Lodge	Maserati 4CL	1st in 1500 cc class
14 July	Albi Grand Prix	Albi	Maserati 4CL	7th
21 July	Grand Prix des Nations	Geneva	Maserati 4CL	4th in heat
10 Aug	Ulster Trophy	Belfast	Maserati 4CL	2nd
1 Sept	Grand Prix del Valentino	Turin	ERA A R1A	Ret'd 3rd lap: gearbox
21 Sept	Circuito di Milano	Milan	ERA A R1A	4th in heat; ret'd in final: back axle
6 Oct	Grand Prix du Salon	Bois de Boulogne	ERA B R8B	Did not start: back axle
27 Oct	Grand Prix de Pena Rhin	Barcelona	Maserati 4CL 1569	ret'd 6th lap: engine

1947

Date	Event	Location	Car	Result
9 Feb	KAK Vinter Grand Prix	Rommehed	ERA A R1A	1st
22 Feb	SMK Stockholm Grand Prix	Vallentuna	ERA A R1A	1st
8 May	Jersey Road Race	St Helier	Maserati 4CL 1569	1st
18 May	Grand Prix de Marseille	Marseille	Maserati 4CL 1569	Ret'd 2nd lap: piston
1 June	Grand Prix de Nimes	Nimes	Maserati 4CL 1569	3rd
6 June	Grand Prix de Reims	Reims	ERA E GP1	Ret'd 7th lap: supercharger
7 June	C. des Petites Cylindres	Reims	ERA A R1A	Reserve to Fred Ashmore; did not drive
13 July	Grand Prix de L'Albigeois	Albi	ERA A R1A	Ret'd 1st lap: piston
20 July	Grand Prix de Nice	Nice	Maserati 4CL 1569 ERA A R1A	Ret'd: selector rod 3rd; shared with Ashmore
9 Aug	Ulster Trophy	Ballyclare	ERA E GP1	Ret'd 12th lap: De Dion tube
10 Aug	Manx Cup	Douglas IOM	ERA A R1A	Did not start
21 Aug	British Empire Trophy	Douglas IOM	ERA E GP1	Did not arrive
21 Sept	Grand Prix de L'ACF	Lyons	ERA E GP1	Ret'd: steering; with Wilkinson
5 Oct	Grand Prix de Lausanne	Lausanne	Maserati 4CL	Ret'd 42nd lap: steering

1948

Date	Event	Location	Car	Result
29 Apr	Jersey Road Race	St Helier	Maserati 4CL 1569	3rd
16 May	Monaco Grand Prix	Monaco	ERA E GP1	Ret'd 22nd lap: engine
25 May	British Empire Trophy	Douglas IOM	Maserati 4CL 1569	Ret'd last lap when leading
? Jun	Bo'ness Hill Climb	Bo'ness	ERA	4th
7 Aug	Grand Prix van Zandvoort	Zandvoort	Maserati 4CL 1569	1st in heat; 3rd in final
5 Sept	Gran Premio d'Italia	Turin	Maserati 4CLT 1593	5th
11 Sept	Hill Climb	Bouley Bay, Jersey	ERA	4th
18 Sept	Goodwood Trophy	Goodwood	Maserati 4CLT 1593	1st
2 Oct	British Grand Prix	Silverstone	Maserati 4CLT 1593	Ret'd 1st lap: fuel tank

10 Oct	Grand Prix du Salon	Montlhery	Maserati 4CLT 1593	8th
17 Oct	Monza Grand Prix	Monza	Maserati 4CLT 1593	Ret'd 17th lap: engine
24 Oct	Circuito del Garda	Salo	Maserati 4CLT 1593	Not known
31 Oct	Grand Prix de Pena Rhin	Barcelona	Maserati 4CLT 1593	2nd

1949

30 Jan	Buenos Aires Grand Prix	Buenos Aires	Maserati 4CLT 1593	Ret'd.
18 Apr	Richmond Trophy	Goodwood	Maserati 4CLT 1593	1st
28 Apr	Jersey Road Race	St Helier	Maserati 4CLT 1593	Ret'd 5th lap: fuel pump
14 May	British Grand Prix	Silverstone	Maserati 4CLT 1593	Ret'd 69th lap: transmission
26 May	British Empire Trophy	Douglas IOM	Maserati 4CLT 1593	Ret'd 5th lap: supercharger
19 June	Belgian Grand Prix	Spa	Maserati 4CLT 1593	Ret'd 7th lap: clutch
3 July	Gran Preis der Schweis	Bremgarten	Maserati 4CLT 1593	8th
10 July	Albi Grand Prix	Albi	Maserati 4CLT 1593	Ret'd 5th lap: valves
17 July	French Grand Prix	Reims	Maserati 4CLT 1593	Ret'd 21st lap: engine
31 July	Grand Prix van Zandvoort	Zandvoort	Maserati 4CLT 1593	Won heat, 6th in final
20 Aug	International Trophy	Silverstone	Maserati 4CLT 1593	3rd
27 Aug	Grand Prix de Lausanne	Lausanne	Maserati 4CLT 1593	Did not arrive
11 Sept	Italian Grand Prix	Monza	Maserati 4CLT 1593	Ret'd 4th lap: big-ends
17 Sept	Goodwood Trophy	Goodwood	Maserati 4CLT 1593	1st
25 Sept	Masarykuv Okruh	Brno	Maserati 4CLT 1593	Ret'd 1st lap: crash

1950

10 Apr	Richmond Trophy	Goodwood	Maserati 4CLT 1593	1st
16 Apr	San Remo Grand Prix	San Remo	Maserati 4CLT 1593	Ret'd 8th lap: mechanical trouble
13 May	British Grand Prix	Silverstone	Alfa Romeo 158	3rd

4 June	Swiss Grand Prix	Bremgarten	Maserati 4CLT	Did not arrive
15 June	British Empire Trophy	Douglas IOM	Maserati 4CLT	6th
24 June	Le Mans 24 Hours	Le Mans	Aston Martin DB2 LML50.7	6th with C. Brackenbury
2 July	French Grand Prix	Reims	Maserati 4CLT	Ret'd 10th lap: engine
13 July	Jersey Road Race	St Helier	Maserati 4CLT	2nd
23 July	Dutch Grand Prix	Zandvoort	Maserati 4CLT	Ret'd 42nd lap: rear axle
30 July	Grand Prix de Nations	Geneva	Maserati 4CLT	Ret'd: driver gave up
7 Aug	Nottingham Trophy	Gamston	Maserati 4CLT	2nd
20 Aug	International Trophy	Silverstone	Maserati 4CLT	2nd in heat, ret'd in final
	Production Car Race	Silverstone	Aston Martin DB2 LML50.7	12th
9 Sept	Italian Grand Prix	Monza	Maserati 4CLT	Did not arrive
16 Sept	Tourist Trophy	Dundrod	Aston Martin DB2 LML50.7	4th; 1st in class
30 Sept	Goodwood Trophy	Goodwood	BRM 151	1st
29 Oct	Grand Prix de Pena Rhin	Barcelona	BRM 151	Ret'd 2nd lap: supercharger

1951

26 Mar	Richmond Trophy	Goodwood	Maserati 4CLT 1593	Ret'd 5th lap: engine
	Chichester Cup	Goodwood	Maserati 4CLT 1593	1st
24 Apr	San Remo Grand Prix	San Remo	Maserati 4CLT 1593	Ret'd 16th lap: rear axle
5 May	International Trophy	Silverstone	Ferrari 375 125C02	2nd in heat 1, 1st in final
	Production Car Race	Silverstone	Aston Martin DB2 LML50	6th; 1st in 3000 class
14 May	Festival of Britain Trophy	Goodwood	Maserati 4CLT	1st
2 June	Ulster Trophy	Dundrod	Ferrari 375	2nd
	Castletown Trophy	Douglas IOM	Maserati 4CLT	1st
17 June	Belgian Grand Prix	Spa	Ferrari 375	Did not arrive
23 June	Le Mans 24 Hours	Le Mans	Aston Martin DB2 XMC76	7th with D. Hampshire
1 July	European Grand Prix	Reims	Ferrari 375	4th
14 July	British Grand Prix	Silverstone	BRM 151	5th

21 July	Scottish Grand Prix	Turnberry	BRM 151	Ret'd at start: drive shaft;
16 Sept	Italian Grand Prix	Monza	BRM 151	Did not start
29 Sept	Goodwood Trophy	Goodwood	Ferrari 375 125C02	2nd
28 Oct	Spanish Grand Prix	Pedralbes	BRM	Did not arrive: car not ready

1952

4 May	Mille Miglia	Brescia	Aston Martin DB2 LML50	Ret'd; gearbox with Gerboli
10 May	International Trophy	Silverstone	Cooper 20 CB152	Ret'd heat 2
2 June	Sports Car Race	Monaco	Aston Martin DB3 DB3/3	Ret'd: con-rod
14 June	Le Mans 24 Hours	Le Mans	Aston Martin DB3 Coupé	Ret'd 2nd hour: transmission
21 June	Formula 2 Race	Boreham	Cooper 20	1st
10 July	Jersey Road Race	St Helier	Aston Martin DB3 DB3/5	4th
19 July	British Grand Prix	Silverstone	Cooper 20	7th
	Production Car Race	Silverstone	Aston Martin DB3 DB3/3	2nd, 1st in 3000 class
18 May	Prix de Beerne	Bremgarten	Aston Martin DB2 LML50	5th
2 Aug	Sports Car Race	Boreham	Aston Martin DB3 DB3/5	Won class
16 Aug	Goodwood 9 Hours	Goodwood	Aston Martin DB3 DB3/3	Ret'd: fire in pits
23 Aug	Scottish Daily Express Trophy	Turnberry	BRM	1st
27 Sept	Daily Graphic Trophy	Goodwood	BRM	2nd
	Woodcote Cup	Goodwood	BRM	3rd
12 Oct	Daily Record Libre Race	Charterhall	BRM	Ret'd: transmission

1953

18 Mar	Sebring 12 Hours	Sebring	Aston Martin DB3 DB3/5	2nd with G. Abecassis
6 Apr	Chichester Cup	Goodwood	BRM	4th
26 Apr	Mille Miglia	Brescia	Aston Martin DB3 DB3/3	5th with L. Klementaski
9 May	Sports Car Race	Silverstone	Aston Martin DB3 DB3/3	3rd

23 May	Sports Car Race	Charterhall	Aston Martin DB3S DB3S/1	1st; debut of DB3S
13 June	Le Mans 24 Hours	Le Mans	Aston Martin DB3S DB3S/2	With P. Collins; ret'd: accident
18 June	British Empire Trophy	Douglas IOM	Aston Martin DB3S DB3S/1	1st
18 July	Sports Car Race	Silverstone	Aston Martin DB3S DB3S/4	1st
23 July	Unlimited Sports Cars	Snetterton	Aston Martin DB3S	1st
22 Aug	Goodwood 9 Hours	Goodwood	Aston Martin DB3S DB3S/2	1st; with E. Thomson
5 Sept	Tourist Trophy	Dundrod	Aston Martin DB3S DB3S/2	2nd; with E. Thomson
3 Oct	Over 1500 cc Sports	Castle Combe	Aston Martin DB3S DB3S/1	1st

1954

24 Jan	1,000 Kms	Buenos Aires	Aston Martin DB3S DB3S/2	With R. Salvadori; ret'd: distributor
7 Mar	Sebring 12 Hours	Sebring	Aston Martin DB3S DB3S/2	With R. Salvadori; ret'd: brakes
19 Apr	Lavant Cup	Goodwood	Ferrari 500	1st
	Chichester Cup	Goodwood	Ferrari 500	3rd
1 May	Mille Miglia	Brescia	Aston Martin DB3S DB3S/2	Crashed
15 May	International Trophy	Silverstone	Ferrari 500	Ret'd heat 2: final prop shaft
	Sports Car Race	Silverstone	Lagonda DP115 01	5th; race debut of car
	3 litre Touring Cars	Silverstone	Daimler	4th; won class
29 May	Two Hundred	Aintree	Ferrari 500	2nd; won in heat 1
7 June	BARC Formula 1	Goodwood	Ferrari 500	1st
	Whitsun Trophy	Goodwood	Ferrari 500	5th
12 June	Le Mans 24 Hours	Le Mans	Aston Martin DB3S DB3S/1	With R. Salvadori; ret'd: gasket
19 June	Crystal Palace Trophy	Crystal Palace	Ferrari 500	1st
17 July	British Grand Prix	Silverstone	Ferrari 500	Ret'd 25th lap: water jacket
	Sports Car Race	Silverstone	Lagonda DP115 02	4th

24 July	Horsfall Trophy	Silverstone	Aston Martin DB3S	1st
2 Aug	August Trophy	Crystal Palace	Ferrari 500	1st
7 Aug	International Gold Cup	Oulton Park	Ferrari 500	2nd
14 Aug	Redex Trophy	Snetterton	Ferrari 500	1st
28 Aug	Joe Fry Memorial Trophy	Castle Combe	Ferrari 500	Ret'd 1st lap: piston
11 Sept	Tourist Trophy	Dundrod	Aston Martin DB3S DB3S/1	Ret'd: accident damage
25 Sept	Goodwood Trophy	Goodwood	Ferrari 500	Ret'd 3rd lap: piston
2 Oct	Daily Telegraph Trophy	Aintree	Ferrari 500	Not classified: transmission
	Sports Car Race	Aintree	Aston Martin DB3S DB3S/1	3rd

1955

7 May	International Trophy	Silverstone	Ferrari 500	Ret'd 10th lap: transmission
	Express Sports Car Race	Silverstone	Aston Martin DB3S	1st
2 Apr	British Empire Trophy	Oulton Park	Aston Martin DB3S DB3S/5	3rd
7 May	Sports Car Race	Silverstone	Aston Martin DB3S DB3S/6	1st
11 June	Le Mans 24 Hours	Le Mans	Lagonda DP166	With D. Poore Ret'd at 8 hours
12 July	BGP Sports Car Race	Aintree	Aston Martin DB3S DB3S/5	3rd
6 Aug	John Brown Trophy	Charterhall	Aston Martin DB3S DB3S/5	1st
	Newcastle Journal Trophy	Charterhall	Aston Martin DB3S DB3S/5	6th
20 Aug	Goodwood 9 Hours	Goodwood	Aston Martin DB3S DB3S/8	Ret'd: hub
27 Aug	Daily Herald Trophy	Oulton Park	Aston Martin DB3S DB3S/8	1st
3 Sept	Daily Telegraph Trophy	Aintree	Connaught B B2	6th
17 Sept	Tourist Trophy	Dundrod	Aston Martin DB3S DB3S/8	7th
24 Sept	International Gold Cup	Oulton Park	Connaught B B1	4th

1956

7 Jan	New Zealand Grand Prix	Ardmore	Cooper-Jaguar	5th
21 Jan	Lady Wigram Trophy	Christchurch, NZ	Aston Martin	4th; single-seater
28 Jan	Dunedin Grand Prix	Dunedin, NZ	Aston Martin	2nd; single-seater
25 Mar	Sebring 12 Hours	Sebring	Aston Martin DB3S DB3S/8	With T. Brooks; ret'd: oil pump
2 Apr	Glover Trophy	Goodwood	Connaught B B4	5th
	Handicap Race	Goodwood	Connaught B B4	1st overall; 3rd on handicap
14 Apr	British Empire Trophy	Oulton Park	Aston Martin DB3S DB3S/5	1st in heat, 11th overall
21 Apr	BARC 200	Aintree	Connaught B B4	Ret'd 5th lap: overheating
	Production Saloons	Aintree	Mercedes B 300SL	1st
5 May	International Trophy	Silverstone	Connaught B	Ret'd 1st lap: gearbox
	Sports Car Race	Silverstone	Aston Martin DB3S DB3S/6	Crashed
	Production Car Race	Silverstone	Borgward	6th, 1st in class
13 May	Spa Grand Prix	Spa	Aston Martin DB3S DB3S/5	2nd
21 May	Race Meeting	Crystal Palace	Connaught B B4	Crashed; broke collar-bone
14 July	British Grand Prix F2 Race	Silverstone	Cooper 39	11
28 July	Le Mans 24 Hours	Le Mans	Aston Martin DBR1	With T. Brooks; ret'd 24th hour
18 Aug	Daily Herald Trophy	Oulton Park	Aston Martin DB3S DB3S/7	3rd
2 Dec	Australian Grand Prix	Melbourne	Ferrari Squalo	Not known

1957

6 Jan	New Zealand Grand Prix	Ardmore	Ferrari Squalo	1st
22 Jan	Lady Wigram Trophy	Christchurch	Ferrari Squalo	1st
29 Jan	Dunedin Grand Prix	Dunedin	Ferrari Squalo	1st

Tim Parnell's races

1958

7 Apr	Lavant Cup	Goodwood	Cooper 45 F2-7-58	Entered but did not arrive
19 Apr	BARC 200	Aintree	Cooper 45 F2-7-58	Ret'd 12th lap: suspension
10 May	Formula 2 Race	Silverstone	Cooper 45 F2-7-58	2nd of five starters
18 May	Formula 2 Race	Brands Hatch	Cooper 45 F2-7-58	11th
26 May	Crystal Palace Trophy	Crystal Palace	Cooper 45 F2-7-58	2nd in heat; ret'd in final: brakes
8 June	Formula 2 Race	Brands Hatch	Cooper 45 F2-7-58	8th in final
5 July	Anerley Trophy	Crystal Palace	Cooper 45 F2-7-58	9th
12 July	US Air Force Trophy	Silverstone	Cooper 45 F2-7-58	1st

1959

30 Mar	Lavant Cup	Goodwood	Cooper 45 F2-7-58	?
11 Apr	British Empire Trophy	Oulton Park	Cooper 45 F2-7-58	Ret'd 30th lap: shock absorbers
2 May	International Trophy	Silverstone	Cooper 45 F2-7-58	13th
9 May	Formula 2 Race	Silverstone	Cooper 45 F2-7-58	1st
18 May	Formula 2 Race	Mallory Park	Cooper 45 F2-7-58	1st
28 June	Formula 2 Race	Mallory Park	Cooper 45 F2-7-58	1st
12 July	Grand Prix de Rouen	Rouen	Cooper 45 F2-7-58	Did not qualify
18 July	British Grand Prix	Aintree	Cooper 45 F2-7-58	Did not qualify
26 July	Trophée d'Auvergne	Clermont-Ferrand	Cooper 45 F2-7-58	10th
1 Aug	Whitchurch Formula 2 Race	Whitchurch	Cooper 45 F2-7-58	3rd
3 Aug	John Davy Trophy	Brands Hatch	Cooper 45 F2-7-58	Ret'd 1st lap: crash
29 Aug	Kentish 100	Brands Hatch	Cooper 45 F2-7-58	Did not arrive; Shelby drove car
10 Oct	Silver City Trophy	Brands Hatch	Cooper 45 F2-7-58	13th

1960

2 April	Oulton Park Trophy	Oulton Park	Cooper 45 F2-7-58	Did not arrive
24 April	Norfolk Trophy	Snetterton	Cooper 45 F2-7-58	Ret'd 1st lap: engine
20 April	BARC 200	Aintree	Cooper 45 F2-7-58	Ret'd 5th lap: oil pressure
14 May	International Trophy	Silverstone	Cooper 45 F2-7-58	Ret'd: overheating

15 June	Grand Prix des Frontières	Chimay	Cooper 45 F2-7-58	4th
1 Aug	Aintree Trophy	Aintree	Lotus 18 FJ	8th
6 Aug	Vanwall Trophy	Snetterton	Cooper 45	Did not arrive
28 Aug	Kentish 100	Brands Hatch	Cooper 45	Ret'd 5th lap: fuel pump
18 Sept	Flugplatzrennen	Zeltweg	Cooper 45	Ret'd
2 Oct	Gran Premio di Modena	Modena	Cooper 45	Did not qualify
8 Oct	Preis von Tirol	Innsbruck	Cooper 45	Ret'd
9 Oct	Coupé du Salon	Montlhery	Cooper 45	Did not arrive

1961

26 Mar	Lombank Trophy	Snetterton	Lotus 18 904	5th
16 April	Preis von Wien	Aspern	Lotus 18 904	Not classified
22 April	BARC 200	Aintree	Lotus 18 904	Ret'd 7th lap: engine
6 May	International Trophy	Silverstone	Lotus 18 904	Crashed 8th lap
14 May	Gran Premio di Napoli	Posillipo	Lotus 18 904	8th; Three Musketeers
3 June	Silver City Trophy	Brands Hatch	Lotus 18 904	7th
8 July	British Empire Trophy	Silverstone	Lotus 18 904	Ret'd 10th lap: spin
15 July	British Grand Prix	Aintree	Lotus 18 904	Ret'd 12th lap: clutch
20 Aug	Kanonloppet	Karlskoga	Lotus 18 904	5th
27 Aug	Danske Grand Prix	Roskilde	Lotus 18 904	10th
3 Sept	Gran Premio di Modena	Modena	Lotus 18 904	Did not qualify
10 Sept	Gran Premio d'Italia	Monza	Lotus 18 904	10th
17 Sept	Flugplatzrennen	Zeltweg	Lotus 18 904	7th
23 Sept	International Gold Cup	Oulton Park	Lotus 18 904	Ret'd 1st lap: fuel pump
1 Oct	Lewis-Evans Trophy	Brands Hatch	Lotus 18 904	3rd

1962

14 April	Lombank Trophy	Snetterton	Lotus 18 P2*	Ret'd 10th lap: overheating
29 April	BARC 200	Aintree	Lotus 18 P2	9th
12 May	International Trophy	Silverstone	Lotus 18 P2	Ret'd 5th lap: oil pressure
20 May	Gran Premio di Napoli	Posillipo	Lotus 18 P2	7th

1963

30 Mar	Lombank Trophy	Snetterton	Lotus 24 P1**	Ret'd 3rd lap: engine
15 April	Grand Prix de Pau	Pau	Lotus 18 917	Ret'd 26th lap: head gasket
27 Apr	BARC 200	Aintree	Lotus 18 BRM P1	Disqualified: push start
15 May	International Trophy	Silverstone	Lotus 24 ?904	Retired 35th lap: engine
19 May	Gran Premio di Roma	Vallelunga	Lotus 18 915	Not classified
28 July	Grosser Preis der Solitude	Solitude	Lotus 24 P1	Ret'd 5th lap: engine
4 Aug	Grand Prix von Deutschland	Nurburgring	Lotus 18 915	Did not qualify
1 Sept	Grand Prix von Osterreich	Zeltweg	Lotus 24 P1	6th, but not classified

* Note that this car was a replica of a Lotus 18 and did not have a chassis number, although it was given the number 'P2' ('Parnell 2'). Chassis 'P1' was driven by Tony Shelly – Reg Parnell's protégé – and was entered by John Dalton, one of Reg's closest friends, who had also raced Austin-Healey 100s and Aston Martin DB3s.

** Again this car was supplied with no number but was known as 952 P1 or 24/P1.

Bibliography

Books
Boddy, Bill *A History of Brooklands Motor Course* (Grenville Publishing Co Ltd, 1957)
Bolster, John *Specials* (G. T. Foulis & Co, 1949)
Gatsonides, Maurice *Gatso – The Never Ending Race* (Gatsometer BV, 1993)
Gauld, Graham *Ecurie Ecosse* (Graham Gauld PR Ltd, 1992)
Gibson, John Eason *Motor Racing 1946, 1947* (BRDC Yearbooks, Motor Racing Publications)
Goddard, Geoff, and Nye, Doug *Classic Racing Cars* (G. T. Foulis & Co, 1991)
Henry, Alan *John Surtees* (Hazleton Publishing Co)
Jenkinson, Denis *Racing Car Review* (various, Grenville Publishing, 1947/57), *The Racing Driver* (B. T. Batsford, 1958)
Jenkinson, Denis, and Posthumus, Cyril, *Vanwall* (Patrick Stephens Ltd, 1975)
Lewis, Peter *Alf Francis, Racing Mechanic* (G. T. Foulis & Co, 1957 and 1991)
Mays, Raymond, and Roberts, Peter *BRM* (Cassell & Co, 1962)
Moss, Stirling, and Hilton, Chris *Stirling Moss, Motor Racing Masterpieces* (Macmillan Publishing)
Stanley, Louis *Grand Prix, The Legendary Years* (Queen Anne Press)
Weguelin, David *The History of English Racing Automobiles Limited* (Whitemouse Editions, 1980)
Wyer, John, with Nixon, Chris *Racing with the David Brown Aston Martins* (Transport Bookman Publishing)

Magazines
Automobile Quarterly (various), *Autosport, Motor Sport, Speed, Top Gear* (Scotland), *Motor World* (Scotland)

Index